Establishing Godly Relationships Through Marriage & Family

Mrs. Deborah Butler

Unless otherwise indicated, all Scripture quotations in this volume are from the *King James Version* of the Bible.

Second Printing 2003

ISBN 1-893575-09-8

Word of Faith Publishing
20000 W. Nine Mile Road
Southfield, MI 48075-5597

Contents

Preface

The material presented in this book comes from years of experience and a practical understanding of God's Word concerning marriage and the family. It is written to fellow ministers and laypersons alike from the perspective of a minister and a pastor's wife, because I recognize the fact that the experience I've gained is not just mine — it belongs to the Body of Christ.

The Bible says in Ephesians 4:11 and 12 that we have a responsibility to share what we have learned to help equip others to do the work of the ministry. And as co-workers in life's vineyard, if we are all working with the same "instructions" — the Word of God — we can get God's work done much quicker.

Of course, there is no way you can take for yourself or act upon everything that is covered, because not every issue presented will apply to your situation. But you can always put a principle on the shelf for future reference and go back over it when you need it.

This is by no means an exhaustive study on the subject of marriage and the family, but I believe the insight you receive will bless and strengthen you as it has me and my family and those to whom I've had the privilege to minister.

Chapter 1

The Wonder Years: Establishing Godly Relationships

Before we can even consider issues about marriage and the family, we have to understand the basic element of any relationship — *friendship*.

We've gotten wrapped up in what the world has to offer, because we think it knows all about friendship. The world doesn't know how to be friends; it knows how to use people, and that's what it has taught us to do. But God wants us to be a blessing to people, not a user of them.

Stages of Friendships

Many of us fail to achieve meaningful friendships because we don't understand that there are different stages of friendships and characteristics and responsibilities that accompany each stage.

There are basically four stages of friendship. Other people might label them differently, but for our purposes, they are the *acquaintance* stage; the *casual friendship* stage; the *close friendship* stage; and the *intimate friendship* stage.

Each stage has its own set of characteristics, freedoms, and responsibilities, which you need to understand in order to evaluate your present relationships.

The Acquaintanceship Stage

The moment you meet or become introduced to someone, you're now acquainted with him or her. You might not remember the person's name, but when you see his or her face, you remember that it's someone you've met. That's an acquaintance.

You may say that the person is your friend after the second time you meet, but he isn't your friend. He's just an acquaintance.

An acquaintanceship is based on occasional contact, such as with classmates at the beginning of a school year: The first, second, or third month, you're just acquainted with one another.

But, eventually, you decide which ones you want as friends and which ones you don't want to know anything else about — *those* people will remain acquaintances. In other words, you can't ignore them when you see them, acting as if you've never met them before. They will always be acquaintances unless you decide to take them to the next stage.

At the acquaintance stage, you have the freedom to ask general questions. For example, if I were to meet you, I'd ask you your name because that's public information. But if I just met you and started getting into your business right off the top, you might decide, *I don't want her for a friend. She's nosy!*

So the distinguishing characteristics of this stage are as follows: 1) *It's based on occasional contact*; 2) *you have the freedom to ask general questions or questions based on public information.*

Responsibilities of the Acquaintance

The *responsibility* that goes along with this stage is that you need to *view each acquaintance as a divine appointment.* In other words, you say, "Okay, Father, why is this person in my life? Is there something You want me to do for him? How should I pray for him?"

You also need to *design appropriate general questions.* For instance, most people don't mind if you ask them whether they're married or divorced. It's public information or something they would volunteer. But some people are so private, you couldn't ask them that as an acquaintance.

You have to take the time to look at each new acquaintance and decide which questions are appropriate and which ones aren't. You can't ask everyone you meet the same exact questions. You have to be able to listen to God and then follow His leading to find out what He wants you to do with each "divine appointment."

The Casual Friendship Stage

When you decide, *I like this person; I want to see what makes him tick*, then you move on to the casual friendship. The distinguishing characteristics are as follows: 1) *It's based on common interests, activities, and concerns*; 2) *you have the freedom to ask specific questions, such as what opinions, ideas, wishes or goals the person has.*

(When I say common interests, I'm not talking about common *experiences*. Common experiences are not a basis for a friendship or relationship. The basis for a friendship is the individual. You should just enjoy being with an individual for the sake of his interests, likes, and character.)

Responsibilities of the Casual Friend

There aren't any *social* responsibilities with casual friends. In other words, you don't have to call or see what's going on with someone. However, you do have two basic responsibilities. First, you need to *learn to identify and praise the other person's positive qualities.*

Too often we major on the negative. That's why some people don't have friends. If you major on the negative, you'll chase people away. You have to find their positive traits and major on those things.

When people come to my husband, Bishop Keith Butler, for counseling, he doesn't just "jump on them" and tell them everything they're doing wrong. He listens and discerns what they're doing right. If he just told them *negative, negative, negative,* they wouldn't come back!

He'll never send you out of his office feeling bad or say, "You're a poor excuse for a Christian — get out of my office" (even though that may be true)! He'll tell you something, such as, "You need to do such-and-such. You're on the right track. We're praying for you; we're in your corner." He'll lift you up and encourage you.

You have to build people up, and you build them up by telling them what they've done right. If you can't do anything else, you can at least call those things that be not as though they were (Rom. 4:17)!

Your other responsibility is to *design appropriate specific questions for children, youth, and adults.* Sometimes we just want to deal with adults and forget about the youth and children. But you can't just ignore them. You have to do the same thing with them that you do for adults, because children are really just little adults. In fact, some children are more adult than the adults are!

Now the general information that you gather as an acquaintance will help you ask appropriate questions at the casual friendship stage. So at this stage, you want to discover what the person is interested in.

The mistake we make is that we ask people about the things *we're* interested in. That's how we make enemies. They might not know we're interested in a particular thing. When we ask them about something that interests us, they think we're asking a legitimate question and trying to get to know them. Then when they give us their honest opinion that they hate something we like, we get mad! So we need to get to know people and ask them about what *they're* interested in.

Most of us have been approaching the friendship from a totally selfish concept — everything is about "me." But that's the world's way of doing things. God's approach is totally different. Everything is about the other person. He's interested in *them*.

You have to show some interest in other people, just like you would if you were looking for a job. Suppose you went for a job interview and you didn't know anything about the company or what they did? You wouldn't be able to ask intelligent questions when they gave you the opportunity.

Hopefully, when you go looking for a job, you take the time to research the company so you can at least look as if you know what you're doing. You want to show your prospective employer that you're really interested in the position.

Well, you have to do the same thing with friendships. When you're working on a friendship, you need to "research" or find out what the other person is interested in. If you just did *that*, you'd save yourself a lot of trouble, because once you found out that someone wasn't interested in what you're interested in, you'd know, *Okay, we can't take this relationship past this stage at all.*

But what we've done is taken folks that were meant to stay as casual friends, and we've brought them into close friendship and fellowship. We've chosen people that *we* think should be our friends, but they *aren't* our friends and can't be.

Because of the way we're conditioned and the lies that TV and Hollywood have presented to us, we'll decide right off the bat, *I like that person. I want him to be my friend.* Then we'll start confiding in that person. But that's how you get in trouble. You may be putting all your information out to someone who will use it against you; someone who is totally selfish; someone who doesn't care about you — he only cares about himself. After you have two or three experiences like that, you'll clam up and won't allow yourself to open up to anyone anymore. And that's not what God intended.

You have to approach friendships God's way, but you have to have some wisdom. You need to be very aware of the people around you, because the same ones who were put in your path for you to help could end up hurting you because you took it too far too fast.

You can't just go headlong and offer people information that they're not interested in. Some people will flat tell you, "I didn't ask you that. I didn't want to know all that." It's too much information. You have to take it slow.

Rev. Kenneth E. Hagin (I call him Dad Hagin) would always tell us when I was a student at RHEMA Bible Training Center that it's better to be too slow than to be too fast. In other words, *it's easier to* catch *up than it is to* clean *up*! You can always catch up, but cleaning up is not so easy.

The main thing to remember is that the choice to move from a casual friendship to a close one is a decision that each individual has to make for himself with God.

The Close Friendship
And Fellowship Stage

From this point on, I'll basically be talking about relationships between a man and a woman, but many of the principles can apply to friendships with those of the same sex.

Close fellowship is something that should be developed at this stage once you decide that a person is someone you want to date and would consider marrying. At this stage, the friendship is *based on mutual life goals.*

Let's say you meet someone, and the two of you go through the casual friendship stage. If you're getting to the place where you feel you want a closer relationship, then you need to begin looking at the person's life goal and how he intends to obtain it.

For example, if he says he wants to be a lawyer, then ask him what school he plans to attend. If he says, "I don't know. What's a good law school?" then what does that tell you? (It would tell me that this person has no intention of being a lawyer and probably isn't going to be anything.) If he hasn't even thought about it, then he really doesn't have that particular goal.

There are specific questions you need to ask before you can take the relationship to the next stage — and don't just *ask* them; *get the answers!*

So the first characteristic of the close friend-ship stage is mutual life goals. Another character-istic of close friendship is *the freedom to suggest mutual projects towards reaching life goals*, which carries with it certain responsibility.

Responsibilities of the Close Friend

The *responsibilities* that go along with this stage are as follows: 1) You need to *visualize spe-cific achievements in each other's life;* and 2) you need to *discern and develop appropriate projects to accomplish those achievements*.

In other words, you're going toward a compati-ble life goal and you're saying, "Let's design pro-jects to help each other reach our goals."

The Intimate Friendship And Fellowship Stage

When you reach this point, you've decided, *This is the person I'm going to marry*, and you're ready to build your relationship on a more intimate level. Unfortunately, what happens with a lot of people is, they'll get married before going through the different stages and then fall out of friendship. Or they'll try to hop from an acquaintance to an intimate friend, and that doesn't work, because there's too much information they missed finding out.

Intimate friendship and fellowship is *based on a commitment to the development of each other's character*. So you have *the freedom to correct each other*.

How many people in your life have the freedom to correct you? Now weigh that number against how many best friends you have. Does it come out evenly? If it doesn't, something is wrong, because your best friend is supposed to be someone that you have intimate fellowship with and who is able to correct you as needed.

If you're married, you don't need a best friend of the same sex. It's nice to have one, but you don't need one over your spouse. Some people spend so much time developing "best friends" that they leave their spouses in the dust, so to speak, and that's totally out of order. Your relationship with your spouse is the one you need to be working on.

If your spouse is not free to correct you, then you have a problem. You're supposed to be helping each other develop God-like character. And I don't care how holy you think you are, you're not there yet. We all have stages of growth that we have to go through.

Now in a lot of cases, the commitment in an intimate relationship is one-sided. The other person is acting like, *It's all right for me to correct you, but you'd better not try to correct me, because I'm all that and more. I'm already there. I don't need any help.*

But we all need help — especially men. (I'm sorry, but if you don't like that, you'll have to talk to God, because He's the One who said men needed a helpmeet.)

A lot of men have a hard time accepting help from women because they haven't gotten rid of the world's ideas about what to do, where to do it, and who to do it with! How can the world tell you what to do? The world has no idea what it's talking about. If the world knew how to be happy, Hollywood personalities wouldn't have so many spouses! It would work the first time.

No one *wants* to get divorced, remarried, divorced, remarried, and so forth. People do that because they are looking for someone to treat them right and with whom they'll be happy. So it's evident the world doesn't know how to find happiness. Yet we look at movies and think, *That's is the way I'm supposed to do it.*

No, that's entertainment. That's just for enjoyment. It's not for you to live your life by. Hollywood doesn't have a clue, because Hollywood didn't create you. *God* created you, and He has the answer to anything and everything you'll face in life. All you have to do is open yourself up to Him, believe His Word, accept it, and do it.

Responsibilities of the Intimate Friend

The responsibilities of intimate friendship and fellowship are as follows: 1) You have *to have open honesty with discretion*; and 2) you should also be able *to discern basic causes of character deficiencies in the other person and suggest solutions.*

That means you don't just point out the person's deficiencies without giving some solutions. You don't say, "I don't want to be your friend anymore because you don't know how to talk to people." No, you're at the intimate friendship stage now. If you don't want to be at that stage with that person, you should have made that decision a long time ago.

The other person has already made the commitment to be open to your correction, so you need to be free to do that. But you also need to use some discretion and tact, which takes time and a lot of prayer.

You have to pray before you can even begin to correct anyone. And oftentimes when you set out to correct someone, you'll find out that *you're* the problem.

Often, we think we're perfect, and anyone who does things differently from the way we do things is wrong. But he's not necessarily wrong. He may just have a different way of expressing himself.

We've let the world desensitize us to the point that we've accepted its way of doing things, and God's way of doing things is foreign. We have it flip-flopped. We need to turn it around.

God's Way Is the Only Way

God's way is the only way to be successful. Without Him, there is no success, no happiness, and no peace — because it all comes from Him. That's why we have to pray about the people He puts in our path and follow the progression He wants us to follow in each relationship.

Following the progression should be just like our relationship with Jesus. When we accepted Jesus as Lord, we were just acquainted with Him at first. Then we entered into a casual friendship. As we spent time fellowshipping with Him, we got even closer. And by cultivating that close friendship, we entered into an intimate relationship and fellowship.

So these stages follow a progression and it's important not to get them out of order. You can't just jump from the first stage to the fourth.

Hopefully, you're beginning to see that developing friendships takes a lot of time. That's one reason why you don't have many close friends. People get messed up because they think they can have five, six, and seven best friends, and they're trying to please them all. They don't have time for seven best friends!

I don't have time for *any* best friends. My best friend is my family. If I have time after my family, then maybe I'll give someone else some time (or maybe I'll just hide and take that time for myself).

Time is a valuable asset. You can't just throw it away on everyone who comes along. And as your priorities change, you'll find your so-called friends will start dropping by the wayside — either that, or you'll have to drop them — because you're forced to reevaluate your priorities and your friendships.

Evaluating Relationships

God doesn't want you to be forced to do it. He wants you to do it on your own. You should naturally begin to evaluate your friendships. You probably already know which friends you need to cut off because you've found out they're selfish. They're not interested in helping you get where you need to go. They're only interested in what you can do for them. That's not a friend. That's an acquaintance.

Knowing how to detect and terminate unwholesome friendships and learning how to develop genuine friendships are two of the most important skills you must have for lasting happiness. So we all need to reevaluate some of our present relationships after we understand what God says is the basic commitment of a friendship.

The Basic Commitment
Of a Friendship

James 4:4 outlines the basic commitment for a friendship. This is a good verse to memorize.

> **JAMES 4:4**
> **4 Ye adulterers and adulteresses, KNOW YE NOT THAT THE FRIENDSHIP OF THE WORLD IS ENMITY WITH GOD? whosoever therefore will be a friend of the world is the enemy of God.**

The Amplified Bible says, ". . . Do you not know that being the world's friend is being God's enemy? . . . "

God tells you right here the basis for all your close friendships. It applies not only to the people you decide to be friends with, but to those you decide to separate from. In fact, you can use it to set the groundwork for the separation. That way you can end the relationship more quickly instead of waiting and making things harder.

That's not to say that all the responsibility falls on you. The other people involved need to understand that they have some decisions to make too. When it comes to letting James 4:4 and your friendship with God set the standard, it's not really your decision that will end the relationship. It's theirs if they choose not to make the same dedication and commitment spiritually that you've made.

You've already made your decision. If they decide to reject Jesus (or to reject moving on with the Lord), which basically means they're rejecting the conditions of the relationship, then they've made their decision. It's not a matter of your being too good for them. You just can't have close fellowship with them anymore.

Sometimes it's hard to tell where you have to draw the line to cut off wrong friendships or let go of people you have outgrown. (By that I mean, spiritually; you and they no longer have anything in common, such as what happens when one person in the friendship gets saved and the other doesn't.)

The Word of God has some specific things to say about the friendships you establish past the casual stage. In fact, there are several scriptures that talk about questionable friendships and wrong relationships, because once you become a child of God, a distinction is made.

2 CORINTHIANS 6:14-18
14 BE YE NOT UNEQUALLY YOKED TOGETHER WITH UNBELIEVERS: FOR WHAT FELLOWSHIP HATH RIGHTEOUSNESS WITH UNRIGHTEOUS-NESS? and what communion hath light with darkness?
15 And what concord hath Christ with Belial? or what part hath he that believeth with an infidel?
16 And what agreement hath the temple of God with idols? for ye are the temple of the living God; as God hath said, I will dwell in them, and walk in them; and I will be their God, and they shall be my people.
17 WHEREFORE COME OUT FROM AMONG THEM, AND BE YE SEPARATE, saith the Lord, and touch not the unclean thing; and I will receive you,
18 And will be a Father unto you, and ye shall be my sons and daughters, saith the Lord Almighty.

2 JOHN 1:10
10 IF THERE COME ANY UNTO YOU, AND BRING NOT THIS DOCTRINE, RECEIVE HIM NOT into your house, neither bid him God speed.

LUKE 6:22
22 Blessed are ye, when men shall hate you, and when THEY SHALL SEPARATE YOU FROM THEIR COMPANY, and shall reproach you, and cast out your name as evil, FOR THE SON OF MAN'S SAKE.

1 JOHN 2:19
19 They went out from us, but THEY WERE NOT OF US; FOR IF THEY HAD BEEN OF US, THEY WOULD NO DOUBT HAVE CONTINUED WITH US: but they went out, that they might be made manifest that they were not all of us.

Now it can be hard to break off a friendship you've had all your life. But there comes a point where you have to make some hard decisions. You have to examine the relationships around you and do whatever is necessary to line up with the Word of God. The Word is your basis for establishing friendships, so your basic standard for every relationship is, if they don't want God, then they can't be your friend!

Sometimes you have to cut yourself off from other Christians too. I've had people actually get mad at me because I wouldn't run with them. As I said, my family was (and still is) my best friend, and I chose to run with them instead.

Once I had to tell one person, "Look, I don't call my mama or *anybody* until I've taken care of my family first." At the time, my kids were growing up and going through different things, and I was spending all of my time with them. So my attitude was, *What makes you think you're so important, demanding so much of my time that I need for my family?*

I have a responsibility to my children and my husband. God is going to hold me accountable for them. He's not going to hold my friends accountable. He's going to hold *me* accountable. I was the one who chose to say, "I do." I was the one who chose to get pregnant and have children. So I had to be responsible for those choices, which meant that all those other things that some people consider so important had to go by the wayside. They weren't as important.

What you have to realize is that some people will try to take their right to choose and force it on you. But just because someone chooses to be your friend doesn't mean *you* have to choose that person to be your friend.

We let people pressure us all the time into doing something because *they* want to do it. Everyone talks about peer pressure with teenagers, but there's adult pressure too. We allow our friends to crowd us or pressure us into doing things we don't want to do.

Questions and Answers

What if I'm married and I become a Christian, but my spouse doesn't?

You can still reevaluate your relationship with your spouse, but the difference is that you can't cut yourself off from him or her. You just have to "pray the situation through." Your spouse and your children are the only ones you can't "throw away," so to speak. But for everyone else, you'll need to separate yourself and limit the level of your relationship if someone doesn't meet the standard that's set forth in the Word.

I know people who have cut themselves off from family members who have reacted negatively to their getting saved. But most of my relatives have avoided me since I've been born again — except for one who wants to come live with me even though he's made it clear that he's not interested in God. What should I do?

Pray about him. He might have been sent across your path for a specific reason. You have to use some wisdom. Don't take what I said legalistically, because then you'll think that you can't have *anything* to do with your unsaved relatives.

As for family members avoiding *you*, you'll find that some people don't want to be around you any longer when you get saved, because they know *they* aren't living right. They feel convicted, but think it's condemnation. So they'll say that you're too spiritual or too good or that you're "holier than thou," which is just a cop-out.

But you also need to check to make sure that you haven't become so heavenly minded that you're no earthly good. When you're "super-spiritual," you don't deal with things practically, and that may be why people want to avoid you.

What happened to being a light to the lost? How can we expect to win people if we "dump" them as soon as we get saved?

Just because a person isn't saved doesn't mean you have to dump him or her. Remember what I said about acquaintances and casual friendships. God may want to use you in a relationship to water a seed that has already been planted. The more water you put on it, the more that person's desire to become a Christian will grow.

Sometimes people are hardheaded and it takes them a little time to come around. Sometimes they're very proud and that's what is holding them back, especially if they've been around the Word and already know what they're supposed to do. When they finally make a decision, they want to make it on their own, not because someone else pressured or pushed them into doing it.

It's like a guy who's interested in the same woman

another man is interested in. If the other man buys her flowers, that guy won't go right out and buy her flowers, too, because he doesn't want to look like he did it just because the other fellow did it. He wants to come up with something original.

That's why sometimes you can be acquaintances or casual friends with people for a long time before they'll eventually tell you they've gotten saved. They'll say, "Oh, yeah. I received Jesus six months ago." But they wanted to make the decision on their own, and they didn't want you know about it earlier because of their pride.

So just keep the friendship casual and stay open to God. You don't want the relationship to progress any further than that, though. If you allow it to become a close friendship prematurely, you can be compromised to the point that the person won't ever come around, or he'll think that you're slipping in your Christian walk.

I understand about confining our relationships with unbelievers, but what's so wrong with a married woman having single friends that are Christians?

There's nothing wrong with it unless you consider them to be your close running buddies. That's different because then you'll be a married woman running around with a bunch of single women, and you shouldn't do that.

Why would you want to hang out with single women all the time, anyway? You have nothing in common with them. They'll talk about their boyfriends, and what are you going to do — talk about your husband?

Someone will end up saying something about what her boyfriend did for her, and you'll wonder why your husband never did the same thing for you. That gives Satan room to create discontentment and discord in your marriage.

So you need to keep those friendships casual. None of them should go from casual to close unless the person involved is just as close to your husband.

What reason can I give to the people I'm separating myself from because they've been hindering me?

Don't be afraid to tell them the truth. People have come up to me wondering why I've "kicked them to the curb." So I tell them: "I simply don't have the time." I'm not trying to be cold, and I'm not saying it to brush them off. I mean it literally, because I've made a commitment to my family, and that takes up most of my time.

But you really don't have to go into detail. Just tell them you don't have the time. It's your choice what you do with your time.

My husband and I are in ministry and we have casual relationships with a lot of people. But certain people desire to have a closer relationship with us than we care to develop. What are your thoughts?

You'll encounter that a lot in ministry. Basically, what happens is that people try to get close to you. They'll tell you all their business and want to be friends with you, not taking your feelings into account. Actually, they're being selfish. They don't realize that you have a choice whether or not *you* want to take the relationship to a different stage.

God has something to say about our relationships and wants to have a part in the relationships we are involved in. As we evaluate our relationships according to God's Word, the godly ones we establish and develop will be rich and rewarding as God intended.

Chapter 2
Developing Stages of Friendships

When you start to evaluate your present relationships, you're going to discover that there are some friendships you need to cut off and some you need to develop. The following are a few basic guidelines that will help you develop relationships at each stage.

The Acquaintance

Be alert and aware of each new person around you. Have a cheerful, friendly countenance — *smile*! Learn and remember the person's name and then greet him by name the next time you meet. Ask appropriate questions that reflect your interest and acceptance, and then be a good listener. Remind yourself of the interest that God has for that person, and it will help you keep the right focus.

The Casual Friend

Discover the person's strong points. Learn about the wholesome desires that person has for his life.

Design and ask specific questions. Show a genuine interest and concern if the person shares his problems with you. Then interchange with him. Be honest about yourself and acknowledge your own faults. For instance, you might say, "I have that problem too" and share what you're doing to correct it. In other words, don't act like you have it on the ball and don't need any help.

Reflect an interest and trustworthiness in being that person's friend, and talk to God about him and his needs.

The Close Friend

See the potential in the person's life and discover and discuss specific goals that he has. Assume a personal responsibility for the development of those goals. Be creative. Design projects that will help the person achieve his goals. Then learn how to build his interest in the projects that you develop. Always be alert to scriptures that will encourage or guide him.

The Intimate Friend

Learn how to give comfort to the person during his trials and sorrows. Assume personal responsibility for his reputation. Be sensitive to traits and attitudes that need to be improved. Discern the basic causes of that person's character deficiencies and help build his interest and desire for correcting them. Encourage him to tell you about your faults, too, and search the Scriptures for keys to a solution.

Finally, make a commitment to be faithful, loyal, and available to one another.

Questions and Answers

Do you have any suggestions about how to maintain a godly attitude toward people who falsely accuse you and constantly cause problems?

You have to walk in love with everyone, no matter what someone does to you. With practice, you can eventually get to the point where the person doesn't even know you're uncomfortable around him, which is really an art. You can't allow his problem to become your problem.

If people have a problem with you, don't just jump on that, so to speak, and start hiding from them and avoiding them. Otherwise, they'll have control over you because they're making you act out of character. Just be who you are.

As for the accusations, listen to what they have to say about you and examine yourself to make sure you aren't doing what they say you're doing. If you are — change. If you aren't, then just keep going on. If they *still* have a problem with you, they just have a problem.

That's the way I handle it. When people say certain things or I hear negative comments about what I've said or done, I have someone whom I trust in ministry that I can go to. That person helps me examine myself objectively. I try to make sure I'm not doing or saying anything that would cause other people problems. But once I've examined myself, I just go on.

You just have to continue to love and pray for those people. Keep the door open so that you can witness to them and bring them up to the spiritual level they need to be on. I've found that those who criticize and talk about you the most are usually the ones who'll come to you when they're in trouble — that is, if you don't mishandle their criticism or tell them off in the meantime!

How does submission come into play in relationships?

In relationships between husband and wife, submission is big. You have to submit all the time in a marital relationship. For example, in First Peter 3:4, the Bible talks about the wife's possessing a meek and quiet spirit ("meek" meaning *teachable* and "quiet" meaning *apt to listen*).

So, first of all, you have to be teachable and able to listen to God. But you have to have a meek and quiet spirit in order to submit to *anyone*. In any relationship where you're teachable and you can hear from God, you're actually in the process of developing a meek and quiet spirit.

I'll talk some more about submission later, but you'll find a quick key in Ephesians 5:21, which says that we need to submit to one another. So it's not just that the wife has to submit to the husband. The husband has to also submit to the wife. It is a two-way street.

Now submission doesn't come into play as much when you're dealing with others of the same sex, but it does play a part to some degree in all of your one-on-one relationships.

Chapter 3

The Primary Years: Laying The Proper Foundation

Once you understand the characteristics and responsibilities of each stage of friendship, you can begin to lay a foundation for dating. Unfortunately, most of us in today's generation don't even know the purpose of dating. Young people are dating just to be dating. Older singles are no better, dating just for companionship or friendship.

I was glancing through a book on marriage one time, and it said that the purpose of dating was to learn how to relate to people. I thought, *Oh, no. If you don't know how to relate to people and you're talking about dating, then there's no hope for you, Honey!*

Relating to other people is something you're supposed to learn as a child. That's what school is all about. You start out as a child, relating to your mommy, daddy, brothers, and sisters. Then you go to school and you learn to relate to all the other children. So if you're dating just to learn how to relate to people, someone along the line did you a serious injustice.

The basic purpose of dating is not to learn how to relate to people and it's not for companionship. It's so you can find someone who is committed to the same life goals with whom you can develop a oneness of spirit.

By the time you decide to date, you should have *already* been relating to one another. At the dating stage, you're working on establishing a close relationship and deciding if you want to take it to the next stage.

Dating

After checking into the tragic accounts of some marriages, it's evident that the decisions and patterns made during the dating process have a far more serious effect on the success or failure of a marriage than most people realize.

Many times people go into the dating relationship unprepared, and they relate to each other in such a negative way. Then they bring that same negativity over into the marriage relationship. Certain seeds were sown during their dating years — seeds for successfully failing in marriage.

They totally destroy their marriage because the relationship wasn't built on knowledge. It was built on presumption, getting even with one another, and all sorts of other little games they learned while dating. So they have the same problems when they get married.

That's why there needs to be prerequisites for dating and marriage.

Prerequisites for Dating

Now the question that I'm asked most often is, "How old should a person be before he or she starts to date?" Well, you shouldn't be dating in the first place if you don't realize that marriage is the ultimate goal of dating! Realizing that marriage is the ultimate goal should be the number-one qualification for dating. Next would be to understand all God's requirements for marriage.

But, generally speaking, you're old enough to date when you've met these four prerequisites:

1. You're aware of both the benefits and dangers of dating. In other words, you've considered its advantages and disadvantages *before* you enter the dating relationship.

2. You've worked out a set of personal dating standards from Scripture, which simply means that, in addition to God's standards, you've established your own personal values for choosing the right life partner.

3. You've purposed in your heart not to lower your standards, even if it means losing dates or relationships.

This last prerequisite is especially important because emotions can pull you in the wrong direction

if you let them. If you're not careful, they'll
automatically decide for you what you'll do in the
early stages of a dating relationship. But most of the
time you don't really see what you're dealing with
until you've been dating for at least six months. By
then, the initial feelings have begun to wear off and
you may find you want to get out of the relationship.
That's when people can get hurt. It's much easier to
set your standards ahead of time and learn how to
control your emotions.

4. *Never, never* date someone you won't consider
for marriage!

The main reason for establishing a set of
standards *before* you start to date is so you can seek
God apart from the pressures and the emotions of
dating. You need that time to determine the sort of
person who will be right for you. Then you need to
settle in your heart that you're not going to let
anything or anyone cause you to lower your
standards. So once you set your standards, stick to
them. You'll both save yourself a lot of time and
trouble by refusing to compromise.

Years ago, our son told us that the Lord had
shown him some things about the woman he was
going to marry. One of them was that our family
would love her.

Then from his own personal standards, he

wanted someone who was from a home that was intact. (Many times when a female comes from a broken home, either she'll be super-aggressive or super-shy — two qualities he wanted to avoid because of his call to the ministry.)

Well, his sisters didn't like any of the girlfriends he'd had, and the one he was seeing at the time was from a broken home and was very, very aggressive. So my son had already begun to lower his standards and his choices kept getting worse and worse.

We had to work with him to get him back on track. (The longer you're out there dating, the more wrong choices you're going to make and the more desperate you'll get, which is one of the dangers of dating.)

That's why it's important to lay the groundwork for evaluating relationships first. You'll avoid a lot of problems if you don't even consider getting close to someone unless that person meets your criteria.

Questions and Answers

What are your personal views on group dating?

One of the misconceptions many young people have is that they need to date one-on-one in order to learn more about a person. But you can learn just as much about someone in a group setting.

I prefer that young singles date in groups, because today you find that teenagers will go out on a date with someone they just met. They don't know anything about the person they're going out with and they can get hurt. So I encourage them to go out in groups.

When you go out with a group of people that you've spent time with and trust, they'll watch out for you. Another thing is that you get to enjoy the company of someone you like without the added temptations that come from being alone with that person.

You should observe the individual whom you're interested in and notice how he or she responds to other people of the same sex as well as the opposite sex. That will tell you a lot. The two things you're looking for are whether or not the person shows respect for his peers and for his parents.

I have a problem with the girl my son is currently dating, and I'm not sure what to do. She is openly rude and disrespectful to me sometimes. It's almost as though she resents the fact that my son is committed to his family. I've come real close to setting her straight, but I've held back because of my son.

Sometimes you have to look past how people act to find out what it is they're *re*acting to. Your case sounds a lot like jealousy to me. It may be that this young lady considers your son to be hers and is trying to protect what she thinks belongs to her. She may also feel threatened that you'll see right through her.

I would definitely pray. If the Lord leads you to confront her, then make sure you do it in love. Just because she's been rude and disrespectful doesn't mean you have to be too.

I don't know what to do with my son. Since he started dating, his whole attitude has changed for the worse. He's like a completely different person sometimes.

Pray. My son wasn't dating at the time, but he went through the same thing in the seventh grade. We put him in a private secular school where many of the kids were snobbish. There was a certain way he had to handle himself in order to function, but he didn't know how to turn it off when he left school. He would treat us with the same attitude that he had all day in school. So I prayed and then sat him down and talked with him. Once he got past his emotions, he listened. But prayer really works. Never underestimate its power.

If a man grew up with his mother making all the decisions and a woman grew up with her mother making all the decisions, it seems to me that they're going to have a problem trying to please each other when they get together. He might let her make all the decisions and then resent it. And she might not respect that fact that she is making all the decisions. How should they work it out?

This happens all the time. They just need to use some wisdom in advance. They should both take turns making decisions about particular matters. However, the husband is the head of the home. All decisions should be made together after communication, but the responsibility of making any final decisions is his.

After a time, they each should feel comfortable in their roles, and, in the process, know what the other one likes and how to please one another better.

I'm dating a young lady who is very close to her father, so I'm sure she tells him things about the two of us. He seems to like me and he involves me with family matters, but I don't feel comfortable sharing with him about my relationship with his daughter.

I respect him as her father, but how far should I go in allowing our private information to be shared?

You're not obligated to tell the other parents what's going on in your relationship, especially since they might use that information against you if they don't like you. There are some parents who don't like you but will act as though they do. I'm not saying that's the case in your situation, but it has happened. (The ideal situation is for the parents to like you, but the most perfect situation is for you to be in the will of God!)

Where her father is concerned, you need to respect him, but you don't want to tell him too much about the dating relationship. Otherwise, he may still expect to hear what's going on after you get married — and that's a whole different area altogether!

On the other hand, you must remember that her father is still her covering, and he still has say and input into her life until he gives her away in marriage to a husband..

I'm a single parent through divorce and I'm dating someone who has also been married and divorced. We're thinking about getting married eventually, but I still have doubts sometimes if the relationship will work. I'm not that naïve to think we won't have our share of problems, and I see some things that could be a potential problem later on. What should I do?

Slow down. Ask yourself the question, *Am I free to remarry scripturally?*Things that happen in a dating relationship tend to carry over into a marriage relationship. That's why second marriages shouldn't be taken lightly. When people have been divorced, they really don't need to get remarried until they know what caused the divorces in the first place.

You both need to understand exactly what part you played individually to contribute to your marriages breaking up and what the Word says about it. Then you can think about getting remarried. Otherwise, you'll only bring along the same baggage that you both had with your previous spouses.

Engagement

The engagement period allows you the opportunity to look at one another more closely once you know you're getting married. It's a time for working on your friendship at the highest level!

Now we said that close friendship and

fellowship is something that should happen in the dating stage. Hopefully, during the dating process, you'll develop a relationship only with a person who meets your standards for life partnership. So if you become serious about someone in particular, it means you've made your choice and you're ready to get engaged. That's when you want to take the relationship to the next stage — intimacy *without* the physical union!

Questions and Answers

How long should a couple be engaged?

That's really an individual matter that needs to be decided by the couple. The mistake that many couples make is that they set the engagement period based on how long it will take them to plan the wedding. Then they get so involved with the planning of the ceremony that they aren't doing what they need to be doing during the engagement process, which is work on the relationship.

Some people say that you need to be engaged at least one year. But don't go get engaged and start planning your wedding for a full year. It doesn't take a year to plan a wedding — not when you know what you want. If you want to wait one year, then that's fine. But base it on your own needs, not what someone tells you. Just be sure to make enough allowances so that you'll spend the majority of the engagement period getting closer to one another and not caught up with the details of the wedding.

My fiancé and I recently had a big fight and my mother keeps prying to find out what happened. What should I tell her? I don't want to lie to her, but I also don't feel like answering certain questions.

You can just say, "We had a disagreement, but we'll be all right." If she still has questions, then you can answer them, but you don't have to elaborate.

Don't alienate your mother. You don't have to tell her your business, but you do have to honor her and respect her.

Prerequisites for Marriage: *Counseling!*

Every relationship is going to take some time, but it will take a little less time if the person comes from a similar upbringing or background because it's easier to understand what makes him or her tick.

For example, if you came from a divorced home and I came from a divorced home, we have common ground there. You basically know what I've felt and experienced by only having one parent in the home.

But suppose you came from a divorced home and I came from a two-parent home. I've been happy every day of my life and you've *never* seen a happy day. Then guess what? You're going to make sure I don't see any more happy days — because you don't know what happiness is!

That's why Bishop Butler teaches that you should marry a "clone" of yourself (someone just like you). A lot of people don't like that. They'll say, "What do you mean marry somebody like me? I don't like me." Well, they shouldn't even be thinking about getting married if they don't like themselves. What are they going to do — go out and find someone just like them so both of them can not like themselves together?

No, you need to learn to like yourself before even thinking about introducing another person into your life.

So premarital counseling is very important. But a lot of times people don't seek it because they're afraid of what will be asked. Some people don't want to come into our office for counseling. They're scared we're going to point out something that they know isn't right, and they don't want us to find out about it.

Their attitude is, *I love her. She loves me. We're getting married.* Then they do the "Vegas" run. Three weeks later they're sitting in our office (some of them don't even last three weeks!). They thought they could work it out, but they couldn't.

Listen, if you think you can work a problem out, then work it out before you get married. You don't have to marry the person and *then* try to work it out. Work it out now.

The silliest thing in the world is for people to get married without counseling, especially when it's available to them. We want people to locate the problem areas *before* they get married. We feel that if a couple comes to us for premarital counseling, it's our responsibility to make sure they know as much about each other as possible. That's why Bishop and I do "X-rated" counseling.

For example, we'll ask all kinds of questions, such as, "Have you ever had a homosexual experience?" or "Have you ever been married before?" If you've been divorced, we say, "Bring in your papers." We want to see them.

We've had couples set a date to get married and their divorces weren't even final! We've had people get married and then one partner finds out that the spouse is head-over-heals in debt. We've even had those who knew they couldn't have children, but they didn't tell their spouse until after they were married — because they were afraid they were going to lose the relationship.

So what we do is make sure people know that before they say, "I do," they'll have the opportunity to say, "I don't and I won't." We also require a couple to date at least a year before they ask for counseling. We want to see if they're really serious about the relationship and to make sure that they're at least friends. The worst thing two people can do is come in for counseling and they're not even friends! You can't be someone's spouse if you're not his or her friend first.

Discerning the Right Life Partner

One of the reasons why so many marriages suffer from breakups and problems is that the couple never laid the proper groundwork, which is something they should have done before they started dating.

Many of the qualifications for choosing the right life partner will be in the dating standards that you've set. You can evaluate each standard ahead of time by asking yourself, *How will such-and-such factor affect a relationship? Will it help build or destroy a marriage?*

Everyone's list will be different because it's based on God's standards plus the individual's personal standards. But here are some basic things that everyone should consider when making up a list.

1. Is the person a Christian? (2 Cor. 6:14)

2. What are my life goals, and is this person compatible with them? (Col. 1:28,29)

3. Does the person have any self-control? (1 Thess. 4:4)

4. How does the person relate to other members of his or her family? Is there harmony at home (because that's how the person will relate to others in *your* household!)? (Num. 14:18)

5. Is the timing right to pursue this relationship? (Gen. 29:20)

6. What is the person called to do, and is that gift and calling compatible to my gift? (1 Cor. 7:32; Matt. 6:33)

7. Am I being comprehensive enough spiritually so that God can fulfill my deepest needs? (1 Cor. 7:36)

The main thing to remember is to set standards that are really important to you and stick with them. That way, when you find someone compatible with your list, you'll know you've discerned the right life partner.

That doesn't mean you should just jump up and get married. Marriage isn't something that you just jump into, because, as I said, you usually don't see what you're really dealing with until you've been in the relationship awhile.

For example, you might be looking at someone who, by the outward appearance, is doing everything right. But you don't know what kind of weeds are mixed up with his seeds! Unless God reveals it to you supernaturally, you'll never know what's really going on with a person until you spend some time with him.

Did you know there are people, especially in the world, who will watch you until they think they know what you expect of them? Once they see you and decide that they want you, they'll become in the relationship exactly what they think you need or want. You're thinking, *This person is an answer to prayer*! and no one can tell you anything different. No one can convince you to slow down.

We've had people tell us, "I don't have to wait, because this is the person God sent me." We say, "Well, if this is the person God sent you, that person will still be there in a year or two. Slow down and take your time." But often they don't; they rush into things because they've fallen for the trap of the enemy.

We've seen it happen again and again. A man or a woman seems to be everything you asked God for —

and the minute you commit yourself, the real person "comes out." Usually, when the enemy sends the "perfect person" across your path, God's person is not far behind. Satan is just using someone else to distract you from the one God wanted to present. So you have to slow down. Take your time. Don't be in a hurry.

If you feel you're in a hurry for anything, that's when you really need to slow down. God will never push you, but Satan will. That applies to every area of your life: God doesn't push you into anything. He'll gently lead you, but He'll never push you.

Questions and Answers

My daughter has been dating a young man from church for some time. I'm concerned that the relationship is becoming serious. He's a Christian, but his personality is all wrong for her. I've tried talking to her about it, but she doesn't see it. I'm not sure what to do at this point besides pray.

When you talk with your child, don't talk about personality. In other words, don't focus on her boyfriend's personality or be critical about it. Take her back to what the Word says and even to what she may have shared that God has spoken to her about the relationship. But keep the conversation off the young man's personality.

When my son started dating, he was making the wrong choices at one point, and we had to get him back on track. We talked with him about what the Word says, what type of person he is, and what he needed in a young lady to complement and complete him. But if one of the girls he was seeing had been his choice, we would have had to shut our mouths and accept her as our daughter even though we thought she was wrong for him. So it's important to talk to your daughter *and* pray.

It is absolutely essential that you pray for your kids. In fact, don't wait until your children are teenagers to start praying about their future mates. Start when they're young.

We have been praying for a long time about the kind of people our children will one day marry. My husband's prayer from the time they were little has been that their spouses would love him. We've already committed these things to the Lord. So now we just have to keep holding on in faith and not get into fear, knowing that our children will make the right choices.

Our son has married a wonderful young woman who fits our family as though I had given birth to her! Our whole family loves her. Tiffany is an answer to prayer, not only for my son, who is truly blessed, but also for my husband and myself.

I'm a saved single woman in my mid-30s. I've been believing God for a mate who is strong spiritually, but most men who fit this description are already married. I've passed up several dating and marriage opportunities with Christian men over this one point alone. Do you think my standards are too high?

First, what most single women don't realize is that the devil knows that God presents the woman to the man. So the devil will try to present you to men who are wrong for you. That's why you have to stay in the Word and have a perceptive spirit about you so that you'll know when God is doing the presenting and when He isn't.

As for your standards, high standards are what you need. You're talking about someone who is going to be your spiritual head. If he's not strong and he's trying to lead you, he'll lead you right into a ditch! So you *should* be looking for someone who is spiritually stronger than you are.

I've known women who were the spiritual giants in their homes. For years, they believed God for their unsaved husbands. (When their husbands finally did get saved, they outgrew their wives so fast, it wasn't funny.) But those were women who were already married. Since you're not married, you should be waiting for someone who can be your spiritual head right now, not later.

You talk about marrying a "clone" of yourself, but how important is it really for two people to have a similar background or common experiences?

Well, it just makes things a whole lot easier, but common experiences are not always a reliable basis for a relationship. Ultimately, the basis for a friendship has to be the individual. That's why you have to pray about the people you come across when you're seeking to establish close friendships.

Just because you find someone who likes everything you like doesn't mean you have a basis for developing an intimate relationship. It's not enough to enjoy being with someone who has the same interests, likes, and character. You still need to have God's wisdom on it. You *always* have to take it to God in prayer.

Chapter 4

The Industrious Years: Building Strong Families

One reason why so many marriages have suffered from breakups and problems is that the proper groundwork was never laid. That's what we've been doing by looking at friendships, which we said are the basis for every intimate relationship.

But now let's talk in terms of love. Your partner in marriage is not just your closest friend. He or she is someone you love with all your spirit, soul, and body. Love is the basis for every strong marriage and family.

The problem with most couples is that they stop working on their relationship as soon as they get married. But you have to continue to work at it.

A Total Marriage

Before you get married, you're working mostly on the soulish level (achieving oneness in soul). Then once you say, "I do," you initiate the physical union (achieving oneness in body).

But you still need to continue to nurture one another as you learn how to come together in spiritual agreement (achieving oneness in spirit). In other words, you're working to build a total marriage patterned after God's divine order — spirit, soul, and body:

Spirit — coming together in one spirit.

Soul — having and maintaining mental and emotional oneness.

Body — coming together in the physical union.

After you're married, God still expects you to work on that relationship. God wants you and your mate to experience oneness in every dimension of your relationship, because that's how He sees you once you get married. He no longer sees you as two; He sees you as one (Gen. 2:24; Matt. 19:6).

In order to build the type of marriage that will bear up under the enemy's attacks, you must develop a oneness of spirit with your mate, because it's only when you're "one" that you can agree successfully in prayer.

For example, if your husband says, "Let's agree that we can do this," and you just give in and say okay, but you don't really want it, that is not agreement. That's called "token manipulation." The minute his plan falls apart, you'll say, "I never wanted it in the first place."

Agreement is when you have discussed the matter, and you both are united in saying, "This is what we will ask and believe God for." Then you will get it every time, because there is tremendous power in agreement (Matt. 18:19).

Now the other side of that is, if you *dis*agree on something, then one of you has to submit in order for the two of you to come into genuine agreement.

Godly Submission

Submission is an act of faith, just as marriage is an act of faith. For example, the wife submits herself to her husband because she sees him as valuable and precious, and she knows that she will receive full provision from him just as the Church does from Christ. But she also submits to him in faith in God's Word.

EPHESIANS 5:22-33
22 Wives, SUBMIT YOURSELVES UNTO YOUR OWN HUSBANDS, as unto the Lord.
23 For the husband is the head of the wife, even as Christ is the head of the church: and he is the saviour of the body.

24 Therefore as the church is subject unto Christ, so LET THE WIVES BE [subject] TO THEIR OWN HUSBANDS IN EVERY THING.
25 Husbands, love your wives, even as Christ also loved the church, and gave himself for it;
26 That he might sanctify and cleanse it with the washing of water by the word,
27 That he might present it to himself a glorious church, not having spot, or wrinkle, or any such thing; but that it should be holy and without blemish.
28 So ought men to love their wives as their own bodies. He that loveth his wife loveth himself.
29 For no man ever yet hated his own flesh; but NOURISHETH AND CHERISHETH IT, EVEN AS THE LORD THE CHURCH;
30 For we are members of his body, of his flesh, and of his bones.
31 For this cause shall a man leave his father and mother, and shall be joined unto his wife, and they two shall be one flesh.
32 This is a very great mystery: but I speak concerning Christ and the church.
33 Nevertheless let every one of you in particular so love his wife even as himself; and the wife see that she reverence her husband.

The Greek word for "submit" can often be interchanged with the word *humble*. It is similar to the Greek word for the God-kind of love — "agape" — because it embodies the same meaning (we'll talk more about agape later). In fact, submission generates or creates that kind of love.

Basically, we can say that submission is determined by the character of the person who is submitting. When we look at submission this way, it makes it much easier to do. The reason why so many people won't submit to each other is that they're looking at it from the standpoint of, *That person doesn't deserve my submitting to him.*

But submission is not based on someone else. It is based on *you* — the person doing the submitting. Whether or not you submit to someone is based on *your* character and *your* attitude toward doing what God has told you to do.

Characteristics of Genuine Love

When I get on the topic of love and marriage, I think of a particular song, "What's Love Got To Do With It?" It's a perfect example of the world's way of loving, which really *doesn't* have anything to do with it! But *genuine* love, *God's* love, is altogether different.

Love is the basis for every strong marriage and family. It's not just an emotion or some abstract concept that cannot be defined. Love is an action — a commitment that is expressed in real ways with certain characteristics that make it clearly recognizable.

If you want to see an example of genuine love, look at First Corinthians chapter 13.

> **1 CORINTHIANS 13:4** (*Amplified*)
> **4 Love endures long and is patient and kind; love never is envious nor boils over with jealousy, is not boastful or vainglorious, does not display itself haughtily.**

Love endures long. It lasts. It keeps on going. It is also patient — willing to put up with anything that's annoying. It displays a calm endurance without complaining or losing control.

Love is kind, doing good rather than harm. It is gentle and considerate in its attitude toward others. It is never envious or shows dislike for what someone has because it wants it for itself. It never boils over with jealousy, dislikes or fears a supposed rival, or feels threatened by others.

Love is not boastful, so it doesn't speak highly of itself or of what it has or knows. It isn't vainglorious, excessively proud, or egotistical. It does not display itself haughtily or feel superior to others, treating them with cold indifference.

> **1 CORINTHIANS 13:5** (*Amplified*)
> **5 It [love] is not conceited (arrogant and inflated with pride); it is not rude (unmannerly) and does not act unbecomingly. Love (God's love in us) does not insist on its own rights or its own way, for it is**

not self-seeking; it is not touchy or fretful or resentful; it takes no account of the evil done to it [it pays no attention to a suffered wrong].

Love is not conceited. It doesn't show too much pride in itself or its ability to do things. It is not arrogant or proud. And it does not have a high-minded or condescending attitude toward others or an exaggerated opinion of its worth or possessions.

Love is never rude, unmannerly, discourteous, or impolite. It will not act negatively or inappropriately. It isn't unbecoming, nor is it unfitting or unsuitable.

Love does not insist on its own rights or way. It is not touchy, irritable, quick-tempered, fretful, worried, discontented, unhappy, agitated, angry, or resentful.

1 CORINTHIANS 13:6 (*Amplified*)
6   It [love] does not rejoice at injustice and unrighteousness, but rejoices when right and truth prevail.

Love rejoices when anything that agrees with God's Word, truth, or spiritual principles prevails.

1 CORINTHIANS 13:7,8 (*Amplified*)
7   Love bears up under anything and everything that comes, is ever ready to believe the best of every person, its hopes are fadeless under all

circumstances, and it endures everything [without weakening].
8   Love never fails [never fades out or becomes obsolete or comes to an end] . . . .

Love bears up under anything and everything. It is always ready to believe the best about everyone and hopes the best for everyone. It knows no weakness, but endures anything. (*See* "Love Is. . ." at the end of the chapter.)

With a "track record" like that, no wonder love never fails!

Four Types of Love

To truly love someone is to commit yourself to that person without guarantee. Therefore, love is an act of faith, and we know that faith works by love (Gal. 5:6); it's a spiritual law.

It is the nature of love to generate love in the life of others: You sow love and you will get love. That's another spiritual law — you reap what you sow (Gal. 6:7).

It's not how much love you have, but the *quality* of your love that's important (just as it's not how much faith you have that God looks at, but the *quality* of your faith).

The love we just looked at in First Corinthians 13 is a certain kind of love: *agape* or *the God-kind of love*. There are four Greek words for love that the Bible talks about: *agape*; *phileo*; *storge*; and *eros*. All four of them have the characteristic of uniting, but *agape* is the highest kind of love.

Agape

As I said, *agape* is *the God-kind of love*. It sees people as being valuable and precious. The quality of this love is determined by the character of the one who loves, not the one who is being loved. That's why God can love us — because His love is determined by *His* character, not ours.

In First John 4:10 we see a prime example of this: *"Herein is love, not that we loved God, but that HE LOVED US, AND SENT HIS SON TO BE THE PROPITIATION FOR OUR SINS."*

God looked at us in our sins and saw us as valuable and precious — worth enough to send His own Son to die for us. No matter what we have done or will do, He still sees us as that way. He loves us.

So *agape* is love that comes from realizing and understanding the value and preciousness of a person. That's why it is called the God-kind of love.

You may ask, "How can I see someone I don't even know as valuable and precious?" You can't, naturally speaking. You *choose* to see that person as God sees him. So if God says someone is valuable and precious, then that's the way it is.

When you realize that, it makes your love walk a whole lot easier, because most of us decide which people we're going to love based on whether or not they love *us*. But the God-kind of love tells us to love *regardless* of how people act toward us. That means we don't have to take things personally.

As we develop God's character in our lives, it enables us to love people no matter what they do to us. We love them because of His character that's on the inside of us.

Phileo

Phileo is *the type of love that you have for a friend.* It consists of that which you see in a person that gives you pleasure. Its quality is determined by the character of the one who loves as well as the one who is being loved (in contrast to *agape*, which is only determined by the character of the person doing the loving).

So if a person doesn't love you, you would still love that person with the God-kind of love because he is God's creation, but you wouldn't want him to be your friend. With *phileo*, the other person's character has to exude love, respect, and some kind of affection toward you, too, since this kind of love is determined by the character of both people.

Now *phileo* works best at the husband-and-wife level and to a lesser degree with children. But it always works effectively with your fellowman as you mix it with *agape*.

Storge

Storge is not found in the New Testament, but it is the word used to express *a show of affection, usually toward children and the elderly*. When you combine *storge* and *agape*, it is very meaningful. However, when you combine *storge* and *phileo* without *agape*, it leads to *eros*.

In other words, when you show affection and love for a friend and *agape* isn't present, it leads to sexual involvement. But if you let *agape* rule all these other kinds of love, you'll be able to keep them in the right order.

Storge is similar to *phileo* in that it works best with your wife or your husband, but it will work to a lesser degree with your children and to an even lesser degree with friends.

Eros

Eros love refers to *sexual attraction*. It only takes on its true meaning when it's combined with *agape* in the marriage relationship. That is the only way it is going to be effective. *Eros* will only work *God's way* with your spouse.

Love and Friendship Paralleled

There are some interesting parallels you can draw when you understand the connection between the different kinds of love and the different stages of friendship. For example, *phileo* gets you out of the acquaintanceship stage into the casual-friendship stage.

Remember, we said that *phileo* is the love you have for a friend, and it is based on your character as well as that of the other person's. So if, as a Christian, your character reflects God's character, which sees people as valuable and precious, then that's how you see the other person too.

Now most dating relationships begin with *phileo*. Then as the relationship progresses and *storge* is added, it leads to *eros* if *agape* is not present. That's why the first thing that ought to happen in a high-level friendship is that you view each other as valuable and precious. You should have that confidence in each other and in your relationship. It will keep you out of trouble.

For example, when two people see each other as valuable and precious, they will not fornicate. The very fact that fornication happens in a dating relationship proves that both parties see each other as worthless. The same is true for the engagement or intimate-friendship stage. Two people can get to the place where they no longer see each other as valuable and precious, and then they will encourage one another to sin.

In review, *eros* is reserved for the marital relationship. That is the only way it is going to be effective.

Storge works best between husbands and wives, but it will work to a lesser degree with children and an even lesser degree with friends.

Phileo is very similar, because it works best at the husband-and-wife level and, to a lesser degree, with children. However, it is quite effective with your fellow man as long as it's always mixed with *agape*.

Agape works best, first of all, with husbands and wives and then with children and other people to almost the same degree. It works well at every level of a relationship because it is the highest kind of love.

Agape — The Building Block of Marriage and the Family

Marriages without *agape* will most assuredly end up in disaster. Couples should always be friends, but you can only build a home on *agape*. *Agape* takes time, work, and patience. (And there is a much better chance of developing it *before* you get married than *after* you get married!)

Sometimes you can think you're operating in *agape* when you're really not, especially if you've been married awhile. For example, in marriage counseling, a wife will sometimes say that she feels as if her husband is putting her down. Then her spouse will say, "I don't make her feel like that." Immediately, he is on the defensive. Therefore, he isn't acting out of real love (1 Cor. 13:5).

You see, in a marriage relationship, it doesn't matter how *you* feel. It matters how *the other person* feels. In the above-mentioned hypothetical case, it is the husband's responsibility to find out why his wife feels as if he's putting her down and then talk it out and fix the problem. That's what it means to operate in agape love.

Agape is not automatic. It's something you have to work on. You have to work on seeing your mate as valuable and precious. You even have to work on seeing *yourself* that way, because you have people telling you just the opposite.

Some people grew up in homes with parents who told them they were worthless and that they'd never amount to anything. So they have to battle that. (This is another reason why it's important not to rush into a marriage relationship.)

Christian woman, if you're dating a man who grew up in a home where his parents talked about him and called him all kinds of names other than the one they gave him at birth, then guess what kind of person you're going to walk down the aisle with!

Do you think that person is going to see you as valuable and precious? He can't even see himself as valuable and precious! He has to work on renewing his mind until he starts to see himself the way God sees him.

Sometimes you can hinder a person from working on what he needs to do by rushing into things. *You* may be ready, but that doesn't mean the other person is ready. That's why it's important to pray about every relationship. The person might be the right one, but God may be telling you to leave him alone —

give him some time and pray that he'll do what's necessary to see himself as valuable and precious. Timing is everything!

Agape in Parenting

Now what we commonly refer to as paternal or maternal love is really *agape*. It is present in both the believer and the unbeliever. The unbeliever is not able to attain to the full level of *agape* because he doesn't know where he got what little he has. He's not hooked up or attached to its source. But the believer *is* attached to the source of *agape*.

Your relationship with your children must be based on *agape*. Eros, phileo and storge will not work.

Ten years ago, no one would have had a problem with that, because almost all of us saw our children as valuable and precious. But today we're finding out that's not true. Some of the things you hear about people doing to their kids lets you know that everyone doesn't see his or her children that way.

You have to realize and understand the value and the preciousness of your home and those who are in it. We dismissed a baby-sitter once, because we came home from an event, and she was on the phone talking about one of our children. If we see our home and our children as valuable and precious, then we're not going to have anyone looking after our children who doesn't agree with that.

Our daughter Michelle has so many different definitions of the kind of baby and child she was because people have told her all kinds of things. They said that she cried all the time and that she was a bad baby. But, truthfully, Michelle was the happiest of our babies. She rarely ever cried. I recently told her, "Look. You just need to stop listening to other people and listen to me and your dad!"

Actually, we didn't have any bad children because we believed that the minute they reacted and responded to the word "no," they were old enough to be disciplined. But we didn't jump on them for every little thing they did, either. We knew they were children, not adults.

You have to let children be children. When you jump on them for every little thing, you're not going to learn the type of personality they have. You'll try to make them like you, and they'll hide who they really are from you. But what you don't want is to have someone around them calling them bad and saying all kinds of negative things about them. You simply can't let people talk negatively to your children.

Communicating Agape in the Home

You can see how integral *agape* should be to the family relationship. As I said, *agape* works best at the husband-and-wife level, then with children to almost the same degree, and then with others.

Your children will never be as close to you as your mate. There is only one person whom you should see as the most valuable and precious person on earth, and that is your husband or wife. Next should come your children, and it is important to make it clear to them that they are valuable and precious through both your actions and your words.

Most men can do that very easily in action, but they have trouble doing it in words. That is one of the problems with the last two generations: Fathers never told their children that they loved them. Likewise, husbands never told their wives they loved them. They just said, "Look at all the things I do for you." But wives and children need to have love communicated to them in action *and* in words. Actions alone are not good enough. Love is something that should constantly be verbally expressed, especially in the Christian home.

In order to have success in your marriage and family, you have to recognize the importance of family (by esteeming the value and preciousness of each member) and establish God's Word as the final authority in your home.

Home and Family —
The Building Block of Society

The home or family is the basic unit of all society. Strong families are important for the success of society and the success of the Church. When you have a society as we have now that doesn't recognize the family, that society will eventually fall apart. And when you have a particular church that doesn't recognize the family or the importance of the home life, you will have an unsuccessful church.

Now the definition of family is *a group of persons of common ancestry*; *a group of persons living under one roof and usually under one head*; *a group of things related by common characteristics and properties*; and *the basic unit of society, having as its nucleus two adults cooperating in the care and rearing of their own or adopted children.*

But I would like to look at the biblical concept of the family.

GENESIS 6:18 (*Amplified*)
18 But I will establish My covenant (promise, pledge) with you, and you shall come into the ark —

you and your sons and your wife and your sons'
wives with you.

GENESIS 7:1,7,13 (*Amplified*)
1 And the Lord said to Noah, Come with all your
household into the ark, for I have seen you to be
righteous (upright and in right standing) before
Me in this generation; . . .
7 And Noah and his sons and his wife and his sons'
wives with him went into the ark because of the
waters of the flood. . . .
13 On the very same day Noah and Shem, Ham, and
Japheth, the sons of Noah, and Noah's wife and the
three wives of his sons with them, went into the
ark.

GENESIS 49:1,2 (*Amplified*)
1 And Jacob called for his sons and said, Gather
yourselves together [around me], that I may tell
you what shall befall you in the latter or last days.
2 Gather yourselves together and hear, you sons of
Jacob; and hearken to Israel your father.

Notice that the family is the vehicle through
which God communicates to man. Also, in Old
Testament times, before the patriots died, they
would bless their children (especially the eldest
son) as we saw in Genesis 49.

So it was through the family that righteousness
and godly principles were taught and spiritual
inheritances were passed on to future generations.

As you read through the Bible concerning the family, you'll find that the family is God-ordained. It is a unit of society that has parental headship and parental discipline. (For example, the Bible tells you to "spank" your child if he needs correction [*see* Proverbs 23:13 and 14]. It won't kill him if you do it where he is supposed to be spanked. We all came equipped with a "spanking spot"!)

Scripture further supports that the purpose of the family is for the establishment and development of God-centered relationships and fellowship, godly character, natural and spiritual reproduction, natural and spiritual dominion, and God-appointed ministry and functions.

So if you want a contemporary working definition of the family, you could say that *it is the God-ordained basic unit of society that has parental headship and discipline and is established for the purpose of enjoying a common life through working, caring, sharing, serving, and ministering to God, others, and itself.*

When you look at the working relationship of the family, you can begin to understand now why you don't have time for all those "friends." What time you do have, you have to put into strengthening the family relationship. Even if it's just you, your spouse, and one child, it still takes time, because the people in your family are changing all the time, and you have to be willing to change with them.

The main thing you need to realize is that you can't change your mate or your children. You have to accept them the way they are and pray for them. Most Christians pray for their families, but then they don't accept their family members the way they are. So their prayers don't work.

For example, a mother can be constantly asking God to work with her child — to point things out to him and deal with him — and then keep voiding her prayers by refusing to accept that child where he is and allow him to grow from there.

You see, you have to let God do the changing. You can't do it yourself. Commit it to God through prayer and then leave it to Him to work out.

I will talk more specifically about children in this next section, but I want to at least mention the woman's priorities in the home first.

Once the woman says, "I do" to a man, her priorities have to come in line with what God has set up for that man. That means, wife, that your *first* priority is to your husband. Your *second* priority is to your children. Your *third* priority is to your job if you're working outside the home. And then your extended family can have a place.

You can easily solve or prevent certain problems in the home by simply keeping your priorities in the right order. Just remember that your job or extended family does not come before your husband or children.

Working With Your Children

As your family grows, you'll find yourself with a full-time job on your hands. Children may be a heritage and reward from the Lord, but they are also *work*! You have to spend the necessary time to make sure that you have taught them, shared with them, and cared for them. And you have to spend the time to teach them how to share with and care for each other. You have to teach them spiritual things as well, such as how to minister to God and exercise their own faith.

So you have an awesome responsibility. It's not just "get married and be happy." It takes work at every stage. And every time you introduce a new child to the family, it is totally different, because now you have another personality in the home that you've never had before.

It is very important that you recognize the fact that your children will all have different personalities. You can stymie the call of God on a child's life if you don't understand and take the time to deal with that child's own unique personality.

For instance, I had always wondered where my youngest daughter came from because she was so different from everyone in the family! Then one day I finally realized that she acts just like my sister. Fortunately, my sister is a Christian.

Your children do not all have to act like you or your spouse. Children are imitators. Sometimes they imitate Dad. Sometimes they imitate Mom. Sometimes they choose to imitate someone outside the home. And sometimes they want to imitate everybody all at once. (Then you really have a mess on your hands. But they'll outgrow that if they're guided properly.)

I believe children should learn from their parents. No one outside the home is responsible for what goes on in your home, so you shouldn't allow others to form your children's opinions. They are supposed to get their opinions, values, and morals from you. And you're supposed to get them from the Bible.

Your children can also learn from you which people are safe to imitate. However, it's your responsibility to find out who their mentors are and to make sure they're following godly role models.

Another thing with children is that you must allow them time to be children. Children go through growing stages, just as we do as adults, so you have to allow them to think.

Talk to your children and ask them questions about different things. Teach them how to think for themselves. And let them talk to you. Listen to them before you "jump all over them" about something. And make sure you're really hearing what they're saying, because it could be something totally different than what you think you've heard.

Whenever punishment is in order, make it appropriate for their age. Younger children need the discipline of the rod, but you need to use wisdom in correcting older ones. You have to get them where it hurts, so to speak, such as taking away their privileges. You want them to think about what they did instead of just being mad at you.

Finally, don't let your children stay home from church. Make them attend. That's part of your responsibility to train them up in the way they should go (Prov . 22:6). Yes, there will be a point where they are just going to church because they have to. But if they keep going, the importance of church attendance and the commitment to make it a priority will "rub off" on them. (Make sure you have them in a good Bible-teaching, Spirit-filled church.)

You can see how building a strong family takes responsibility and discipline on your part — in other words, *work*! But the rewards are worth the time you invest in your greatest asset in life, your family.

The following is from a handout called "Love Is. . . " that I give to the students in our Bible training center. It's based on First Corinthians 13:4-8, and it's a vivid description of what genuine love is. Read it, meditate on it, and get it in your spirit. Then apply it your life, especially in the home.

Love Is. . .

Love endures long, (lasts, keeps on going) and is patient, (willingness to put up with waiting, or anything that annoys; calm endurance without complaining or losing self-control), and kind, (doing good rather than harm, gentle, considerate attitude toward others). Never is envious, (being or showing dislike of what someone has because of a wish for what the person has). Never boils over with jealousy (a dislike or fear of supposed rivals, envy, a feeling of being threatened concerning something that's yours).

Does not act unbecomingly, (not fitting, suitable or appropriate). Love does not insist on its own rights or its own way, for it is not self-seeking. It is not touchy (irritable, quick-tempered), fretful (worry, discontent, peevish, unhappy, agitated), or resentful (to feel injured, angry, insulted); it does not keep a record of the evil done to it, pays no attention to a suffered wrong. It does not rejoice at injustice (an unjust act or circumstance or wrong), and unrighteousness (sinful conduct); but, rejoices when right (anything in line with God's Word) and truth (anything agreeing with spiritual law set up by God) prevail (to exist, be general standard). Love bears up under anything and everything that comes, is ever ready to believe the best of every person. Its hopes are fadeless under all circumstances, and it endures everything without weakening. Love never fails, never fades out, or becomes obsolete, or comes to an end. Love respects authority.

Love is not boastful (speaks highly of oneself, of what one owns or knows; to brag) or vainglorious (excessively proud or boastful, egotistical), does not display itself haughtily (feeling oneself superior to others and showing it by treating them with cold indifference and scorn). It is not conceited (too much pride in oneself or in one's ability to do things), arrogant (proud and showing an attitude of highmindedness to others) or inflated with pride (high opinion of one's own worth or possessions). Love is not rude (unmannerly, not courteous, impolite, a negative way of acting).

Chapter 5
The Turbulent Years: Overcoming Life's Crises

Change is an inevitable part of life. Without it, we'd become stagnant. But it's how we handle life's changes that determines our success or failure, especially in the time of crisis.

A crisis is a turning point — a point of no return, where a critical decision must be made. Making the right one will open the door for growth and prosperity. But making the wrong one can set you back years or destroy everything you've worked so hard to achieve.

According to the dictionary, a crisis is *an emotionally significant event or radical change in a person's life*. It's *an unstable or crucial time in which a decisive change is impending with the distinct possibility of a highly undesirable outcome.*

Mid-Life Crisis

Mid-life crisis (MLC) is a term used to describe the series of traumatic changes and events that come during middle age. It's a time of high risk for marriages and can be a time of depression, anger, frustration, and rebellion.

MLC affects the physical, social, cultural spiritual, and occupational expressions of your life. It may affect just two or three of these areas or all of them at the same time.

If a situation arises that affects just one of these areas, that's not necessarily MLC. That's just a change you go through in life. All of us have small crises in our lives. But when several of those areas are affected all at once and you have to make a crucial decision that could change the rest of your life — *that's* MLC!

A lot of people get to this point and want to rush into a decision. So they'll try something, and if it doesn't work out, they'll try something else. But you have to slow down and think things through. You want to be sure you're making the right decision, because it will definitely have an impact on the rest of your life.

MLC may manifest suddenly and result in a career disruption or an extramarital affair. A man might decide to quit his job and start a new career, or he might be laid off and have to make a decision about what to do with the rest of his life.

If his wife is not doing what she's supposed to be doing at home, he may begin to pursue interests or involvements outside the marriage, because he feels he needs to prove that he's still a man and still desirable. It doesn't mean he's going to leave his wife. It just means he has a need that needs to be filled, and since she isn't fulfilling it, he may find someone who will.

Some men leave their commitments because they're in denial. They're blaming others for the crisis instead of looking at themselves. You see this happening with men who blame their wives for everything and then dump them for younger women.

Sometimes they leave because they've examined their lives, and all they could see was that they'd been "trapped" into a relationship. (Of course, when they were in their twenties, they didn't look at it as being trapped. But now, all of a sudden, they feel they were forced into the relationship.)

You hear stories of people who go through MLC and become a totally different person. They just jump up and leave their families, never to be heard from again. Women do it too.

I know a woman who left her husband and five kids and started a whole new life. I can't understand a mother leaving her children. I have tried for years, but I can't! Seriously, I could see her feeling like she has to get away from her husband, but I can't understand her leaving her children. Yet it does happen.

Generally, women handle MLC a little better than men do because they're more emotional beings. They have to change and adjust themselves so often in life that they're used to dealing with things on an emotional level.

Men, on the other hand, are mostly physical beings. They're not used to dealing with emotions, and this is a time of their lives that is very emotional. They just can't handle it. That's why you'll see different manifestations of extreme behavior in some men. They'll change their job, start dressing like a teenager — do all sorts of radical things to recapture something that they used to have. They'll regress, trying to find their youth. Old men will even marry young women half their age. Now you tell me, what can an 85-year-old man do with a 35-year-old woman — besides die happy!

When Does Mid-Life Crisis Come?

It's difficult to determine exactly when MLC will occur in someone's life, because it's brought on by his experiences. It's not based so much on chronological age as it is the person's state of mind. So it will vary.

I believe my husband and I went through MLC at a very early age because of the things that have happened in our lives. We've had an opportunity to grow and mature in a lot of areas that some people are just now experiencing. Sometimes when we share about what's going on in our ministry, people think that we're older than we really are.

You see, your chronological age may be 40, but your life experience might be equal to someone who is 50 or 55. So it doesn't have to do with chronological age. It has to do with what kind of goals you've chosen in life, your experiences, and how you handle developmental problems.

Some people reach the goals they've set for their life by age 30. Then they're thinking, *Where do I go from here?* Depending on how they've trained themselves to handle problems, reaching a goal that they thought would take all their life to accomplish could trigger a crisis.

Can you imagine a 30-year-old talking about feeling useless, his life being over, or not knowing what he should do now? You're wondering, *What's his problem?* And you want to tell him, "Then just set some new goals!"

Now for women, MLC usually happens in their late-30s to early-40s, and it can be brought on by life experiences, such as the empty-nest syndrome.

(We'll talk about that in another chapter.) Some women experience MLC the same time as menopause, but most will go through it much earlier than that.

On the average, men will experience MLC during their early-to-mid 40s, which is usually the time when they begin to reexamine themselves. A man will first examine himself at around age 29 or 30 to see whether or not he's set personal goals for himself. But it's not as severe as when he reexamines himself in his 40s.

This time he'll ask himself questions, such as: *Am I fulfilled? Have I achieved what I wanted to achieve in life? Am I happy where I am?* and so forth.

At 30, most men are just getting their start in life, so it's too early to ask those things. But once a man hits his 40s, he begins to look on the other side and think, *My life is half over and what have I achieved?*

Doubts and Questions

One reason why MLC is such an emotional time is that your soul or mind is under assault. Your human will is being tested and your thoughts are constantly plagued with doubts and questions.

The four basic areas that people in MLC always tend to question are the *purpose of life*, their *choices in life*, their *relationships*, and their *worth as a person*.

'Why Do I Exist?'

This is usually the big question, and you'll never come up with a constructive answer apart from the Word of God.

Why am I here? This question usually leads to doubts and questions about a person's choices of environment, neighborhood, church — *Do I want to live in this house? Do I want to live in this city? Do I want to go to this church?* and so forth — even though nothing may be wrong with those choices.

You might want to change your environment or go somewhere where no one knows you and start over again. The world is telling you, "You need a change." But it's trying to force you to make the wrong changes. And if you take it to the extreme, you might drive off one day and leave the city or even the country.

'Do I Want To Be In This Family?'

A lot of couples decide at this point that they don't want to be married anymore. They don't have a reason — they just don't want to be. People who really love each other have split up that way. They were at the point where they wanted a change, but they were so narrow-minded that the only way they could see a change coming about was to go separate ways.

Some people will go through a time of deep depression and start having what I call "stupid, off-the-wall" thoughts, such as, *Why did my parents have me? I should sue them, because I didn't ask to be here.*

Now that's crazy! How were they going to ask their parents in the first place!

'Who Am I?'

This is when you start examining yourself, asking: *What am I about? Why couldn't I be someone else?* The doubts and questions in this category feed on your feelings of insecurity, and you could eventually get to the place where you don't even know who you are anymore.

Recognizing MLC

Now we know that it is possible for Christians to go through *any* crisis victoriously. But you have to first recognize the problem. There are people who've experienced MLC but never put a name to it because they didn't recognize it for what it was. They just figured they were going through a very hard time in their lives. But there are certain symptoms to look for in order to identify MLC when it comes.

Symptoms of MLC

You can expect to experience outbursts of anger, deep depression and withdrawal, instability, confusion, sulkiness, rebellion, and especially frustration — you become frustrated about everything. Those are just some general symptoms, but there are three major forces that usually bring them on.

Biological Changes

Biological changes include the natural changes that occur as a result of the aging process, such as a shift in body weight and the loss of vigor, muscle tone, skin tone, or hair. Depending on the type of person you are, these things can be very traumatic and become a triggering factor for MLC.

The "big three" changes in appearance will be in your hair, skin, and weight. You'll look at your hair one day and realize that it's the wrong color — it's turning gray or white. If your hair is falling out, you may start to wear a toupee or wig. You'll also notice changes in your skin: it might be getting harder in spots. But for the most part, it will begin to get loose or flabby. (Good-bye tight skin!) Your weight and your body metabolism will also start to change.

Now it doesn't matter what you do, these things are going to happen. There are some natural measures you can take to help so that you don't look as bad. You can slow down the aging process by exercising, eating right, and taking care of your skin. But your body is still going to change, because it's deteriorating as you get older.

It's perfectly natural to want to take care of your appearance. But when you go to the extreme and the way you look becomes the most important thing in your life, you may be facing MLC.

Your Psychological Makeup

Your ego and self-image are components of your psychological makeup, which plays a large part in the decisions you make. Usually, if you have a weak psychological makeup, you'll also have a low self-esteem, which means you're more likely to make destructive decisions about the choices you're faced with.

You also tend to take things personally. You either blame yourself for everything or you blame everyone else and never take responsibility for anything.

Now if you never deal with why you have such a negative perception of yourself in the first place, you'll keep falling back into the same pattern of negative thoughts and behavior. You won't believe anything good that anyone has to say about you. Someone could give you a compliment and you'd think he was lying or kidding. But if that same person told you something *negative*, you'd believe it and say, "Yes, I know. I'll try to be better." It doesn't make any sense, but that's what a bad self-image will do.

You also are highly impressionable and may value other people's views and opinions above your own. For example, you may meet a person who says he's an expert on the job market, and he tells you a bunch of negative things about the occupation you're in. You may come away from that conversation and adopt that person's views.

If you take it to the extreme, you may make a decision to change careers because of the impressions you came away with that day. Then years later, it catches up with you when you realize that you're in a job that you don't even like. Well, now you have a major problem — especially if you're in your latter years.

Social Influences

Social influences are very strong forces that contribute to MLC, because you're not only dealing with your own personal struggles but the world's social values as well — and the world is basically saying that life isn't meaningful after 40. (If you notice, that's the general age range of MLC.)

The messages you receive all say, "You're no good anymore. It's over. It's all downhill from here." And they're coming from every segment of society. Television advertisers promote the image that youth is good and aging is bad. Hollywood basically says, "If you're young, we want to use you. If you're old, go somewhere and die."

Some veteran actors get older and the producers put more wrinkles on them. They get treated like a bouquet of old flowers: *Why keep them around? They're no good anymore. They look like they're about to fall apart anyway, so just throw them in the garbage.*

That's what we do with our elderly folks. Society looks at them and says they're no good; they're no longer useful; they don't count. So we put them away somewhere to die. We don't want to listen to them anymore. And Satan steals from us a precious resource, because they have some wisdom that we need.

Now these are just a few of the social influences that you have to guard against, because society will make you feel rejected and have you reevaluating your relationships with your wife, children, colleagues, friends, and even God — and you should *never* let anything or anyone make you question your relationship with Him.

It's a 'Woman' Thing

Before we look at strategies for preventing and dealing with MLC, I want to focus for a moment on the woman. As women, we face some specific pressures that produce stress and can trigger a crisis in mid life.

Cultural Views of Women

Adversities affecting every aspect of our lives are going to come, especially during MLC. So we need to learn to appreciate what we have now instead of looking back and longing for something we once had. You can't turn back the clock or change the past, but you can make quality decisions that will help keep you stable and productive throughout your latter years.

One of the first decisions you need to make is to stop listening to what society tells you. Why is it that when you're young, you don't care what society says. But as you get older, you begin looking at what society is saying about you?

You'll see all those young actresses on television and get mad, thinking, *What do they have that I don't have?* Youth! But you have (or should have) something *they* don't have — the wisdom that comes with age.

Aging is a process that God set in motion. Personally, I'm not ashamed of my age. In fact, I don't understand why Christian women don't want to tell their age or feel they have to lie about it, because God has promised us long life.

When I tell people my age, I'm saying: "This is how long I have lived so far, and this is how much longer I have to go." That's what age means to me. Every time I tell my age, it reminds me that God has been faithful.

There's no need to lie about your age. You should tell it proudly because it's a witness.

Marital Issues

Marriage is another major cause of undue stress for women. For some, it's the lack of marriage that is causing the stress. If your knight in shining armor hasn't shown up yet, then use your time constructively to examine yourself. Don't worry about trying to examine others. Just make sure that you're where God wants *you* to be.

Now some women are dealing with being

unhappily married. There is no point in worrying or getting stressed out because you're dissatisfied and your marriage is in trouble. You need to redirect your focus. Try putting the same amount of energy that you spend on dealing with the stress into correcting the situation. Start looking in the Word of God for the solution instead of worrying about where you missed it!

Sometimes we get lazy and we don't want to do these things. We think, *I'm a woman, so I should know what to do.* But we really don't know. That's Hollywood talking. Only God knows what to do. He knows our mates better than they know themselves. God can tell us exactly what to do to fix any situation and when to do it. And He will share it with us if we go to Him!

If you're facing divorce, your number-one obligation or duty is to make sure that you're doing everything God requires of you so that if the divorce decree is signed, you're at peace, because you know that you've done what God said. Otherwise, you'll wind up beating yourself up over your divorce for the rest of your life.

When a woman who has gone through a divorce comes in for counseling, I encourage her to be upfront with me. I've seen too many women repeat the same mistakes over and over again because they were in denial: It was always "*his* fault." So I ask them point-blank, "But what did *you* do?"

Divorced women who want to remarry need to be honest with themselves to see where they made the mistake the first time. That's the only way they're not going to make the same mistake a second time.

Career Priorities and the Biological Clock

Two more stress-makers for women are the pressures of career and our biological clocks that constantly remind us that soon it will be too late to accomplish our lifelong dreams. This is a category where a lot of single women get into trouble.

For years, their number-one commitment was to their profession and advancing their career, so they didn't have time to get married. But now that they've achieved some degree of success, they're ready to settle down.

Or they may want to get married and become a mother because they're getting old. So they rush into a relationship. They sensed the urgency of their inner clock, and it forced them out of God's timing and right into the arms of a disaster.

It's the world that sets limits on what age you can do things. If getting married and having a baby is a desire of your heart, then just believe God and wait on Him. If He could do it for Sarah, He can do it for you. Of course, you probably don't want to have a baby in your 90s, but the point is, God is not a respecter of persons (Acts 10:34).

'Colliding Emotions'

Another experience that is hard to describe has to do with the turbulent struggle that is taking place inside of you. I call it "colliding emotions."

Colliding emotions are a rough, explosive, crisis-type transition, a quiet restlessness, and an inner confusion — all at the same time. In other words, total mass confusion! You say, "How can that happen?" I don't know, but it does.

You may have experienced something like it if you've ever dealt with a little baby while you were mad at your husband. You're playing with the baby, talking baby talk, and then your spouse shows up. All of a sudden, you find yourself arguing and hollering at him and playing with the baby at the same time.

Or maybe you've been in the middle of an argument when the telephone rang, and you picked up the phone and said hello, sounding like the happiest person in the world. Then you hung up the phone and started arguing again. Well, those are examples of colliding emotions.

Now take that and multiply it by a hundred, and you'll get an idea of the conflict you're dealing with when you go through MLC. MLC is a hundredfold, all-out war on your emotions!

Loss

Another factor is the accumulation of traumatic losses. You'll find that as you get older, there will be more and more losses that you have to deal with, such as the death of extended family members or friends (especially those your age). Often when this happens, you begin to reassess your life and wonder, *Oh, no. Am I next?*

Another dimension of loss aside from death is the loss of someone or something familiar. It may be that the children are grown and have left the house or that you're facing retirement or were laid off from your job. Any type of loss can create a vacuum in your life, which can bring about MLC.

Children

Women who have kids are also subject to the added pressures that come from their children's growing demands and eventual independence. This is something that I believe contributed to my going through MLC when I was in my 30s.

My children were still in the home, but they

were very independent. I had already taught them how to do laundry, wash, cook, and whatever else they needed done besides iron. (I don't buy clothes that you have to iron.) So they really didn't need me to do anything for them.

Basically, all I was doing was making sure they did their chores — and even then, all I had to do was say, "I'm telling your daddy," and that was it. It was taken care of. So all they really needed was someone to drive them around to different places. And that didn't even need to be me, because I could have just as easily called them a taxi! So I really felt useless.

I was beginning to experience a mid-life crisis, and I went through a time of self-examination. I thought, *Well, I've had my children and they're all grown now; they're at an age where they don't need me. Maybe I've done too good a job in bringing them up.* Then on top of all that, I had forgotten about the calling of God on my life.

Well, one day I was out shopping with my brother and his wife, and I came across this T-shirt that said, "It's my mid-life — I can crisis if I want to!" I grabbed it immediately. I really bought it out of self-pity at first, because I'd put it on whenever I felt like saying, "Just leave me alone! I'm crisising right now!"

I mean, I was at a point in my life where I felt like screaming at the top of my lungs. I was literally overwhelmed. I just wanted to get in the car, drive off, and never come back. I'd think, *Just go and keep on going.* I didn't even have a destination in mind. I just thought anywhere would be fine, as long as it wasn't "there."

It seems totally stupid now when I think back on it, but that's honestly how I felt. I just didn't want to be there anymore. It didn't have anything to do with anyone else. It was just me "crisising."

One day, I was looking at that T-shirt, and it was if I actually read it for the first time. This time when I saw, "It's my mid-life — I can crisis if I want to," I decided that I didn't want to. That's what helped me get over it: I didn't *want* to!

I got up and went where I should have gone in the first place — to God! I said, "Lord, I know that I can do all things through Christ who strengthens me [Phil. 4:13]. So if I don't want to crisis, I don't have to crisis, because You give me the strength not to."

You see, God's Word was the answer all the time. I was going around frustrated, trying to reexamine all the things that were making me feel the way I did, when all I had to do was get into the Word of God, make the adjustment, and go on to the next phase of my life.

You don't have to stay in one area all your life. That's what the devil and the world tries to make you think. They'll try to put you in a box and say, "You have to do this, and it's the only thing you can do." No, it's not. God is your Creator. *He* tells you what you can do.

In my case, I knew I had a calling on my life, and that's what He brought me back to. But I also knew that there were priorities I had to keep in order to flow into that calling. My first priority was to my husband: Whatever he needed me to do, I needed to do. At the time, he was traveling and was busy with the church. So he needed me to be home with the children. That was my priority. That was my first calling — to be with my children, to be there for him, and to be there in the home.

Then when my children didn't need me at home anymore, I was free to go help out in the church and do the things my husband needed done there. The busier he became, the more I needed to be at the church.

Now that my children are older, they're getting to the point where they're able to help out in the church. So I'm finally free to travel with my husband. But I would have never gotten to this stage if I hadn't made the right choice at that critical juncture in my life.

I held onto that T-shirt for a long time to remind me of where I was back then and where I am now. It was meditating on what it said that finally got my attention long enough to realize that I could decide what I wanted to do about the crisis. But it was taking my decision to God and doing what the Word said that actually brought me out.

If I ever have to deal with another crisis again, I won't have to go through that because I know what to do. Actually, if I continue to examine myself every day, I won't have to go through another crisis because then I won't allow things to "pile up" on me.

A crisis only happens because people let problems pile up on them. You can't keep putting problems away in neat little corners and say, "I'll take care of them later." If you don't, you'll wake up one day and suddenly discover that all those problems need to be taken care of right then, all at the same time. And then you'll have a crisis for sure!

Chapter 6
Mid-Life Without the Crisis

In the last chapter, we talked about the "mid-life crisis" or MLC and some of the stressors of middle age that can bring it on. In this chapter, I'm going to talk more in-depth about how to deal with MLC scripturally once it hits and even how to prevent the temptation of MLC from ever becoming a crisis in your life.

One thing everyone wants to know about MLC is how long it lasts. That depends on how you deal with it! Some people may be able to handle it in a matter of a week and some could even probably do it in a day. It may take others a few months to get through it, and, some, years because they're in denial. They either don't want to face it or they don't want to admit they're going through MLC.

Then there are those few rare cases of people who go into MLC and never seem to come out of it. They just pitch their tents and set up camp. But you can't just stay in it. You have to go in and go out. That's why they call it "going *through* mid-life crisis"!

Now for the Christian, MLC is something that you don't have to go through. I'm not saying that it won't happen, but the level of crisis depends on your prayer life. In other words, it doesn't have to be a negative thing or something that destroys your life, especially if you spend time in prayer and handle it according to the Word of God.

Some people have come up on MLC, but because they had a strong prayer life, the Holy Ghost would tell them what to do, so they were able to sidestep and avoid a lot of the things we've been talking about. It wasn't a crisis for them after all, because their whole attitude about it was different. They looked at it as a challenge, an opportunity to do something else with their lives that they've always dreamed of doing.

When you try to deal with MLC according to the world's standards, it can be a very negative experience. But when you examine yourself and do the things that the Word instructs you to do on a daily basis, when MLC comes, you'll find yourself going straight through it.

Survival Traits

A survey was given to couples experiencing MLC, and the following traits were what they listed as crucial keys to their holding their marriages together.

1. A commitment to stay married and to keep their marriage as a high priority

2. The ability to communicate
3. A personal spiritual life
4. The ability to resolve conflicts
5. Relationships with other people
6. Sexual intimacy
7. Sharing fun, leisure, and humor
8. Realistic expectations
9. Serving each other and sharing leadership
10. Growing personally

Preventive Measures

As we said, you don't have to have a crisis if you know what the Word has to say. But there are a few practical things you can do to help take the "crisis" out of mid-life crisis.

First, you need *to identify the seed problem*. The feelings that surface in MLC are usually the by-product of a deeper problem. For example, if you say, "I'm not where I should be or wanted to be by now," you've only expressed the frustration. But if you recognize that you haven't obtained your goals because you never finished your schooling, then you've just identified the seed problem.

Second, you have *to communicate your needs*. Communication is very important. For instance, you could tell your spouse, "Honey, we got married so early that I never got to finish college. I would really like to go back to school." It may surprise you to find that when you communicate your needs, your spouse will be in agreement with you.

You need to be able to tell others what is happening in your life, so you should find someone you trust to talk to. The best person is not a friend. It's usually a minister or your spouse. Depending on what the seed problem is, you might want to talk to your spouse in front of a minister.

Third, you have *to do something to make up for the deficit or sense of lack that you're feeling in your life.* After you identify the seed problem, you need to make a decision what to do about it. If it's career reentry that you desire, go back to school and get your degree (even if you have to take one class at a time). If it's attention that you're lacking, get a new haircut or try a new look. If you're going bald, shave your head and shine it up good! Whatever you decided to do, go for it.

Fourth, always strive for balance in your life. Stay on the middle road. One way to keep balance in your relationship is by serving your spouse and sharing the leadership role. Sometimes when a partner goes through a crisis, he or she doesn't want to make the decisions. That's when you need to step in. You need to help share the load.

You can also help your spouse through this time by being extra supportive and seeking to continually grow with him or her personally, not just spiritually. This is crucial in a marriage, because many times you'll have one spouse who is growing personally while the other one stays at the same level, which happens many times with wives who stay at home.

Their husbands work and they're home with the children. He's out in the work force, interacting with people, reading the newspaper, and so forth. And she's stuck in the laundry room, interacting with the baby, and reading homework papers. The husband is growing, and the wife is left behind. (That's why a man sometimes gets personally involved with his secretary — because the secretary has to constantly stay at a close level with him intellectually to know what he's talking about.)

So the husband comes home and his wife wants to talk about what the kids did all day. He wants to talk about the decisions he has to make at work tomorrow. He doesn't want to hear about the kids, which is wrong, and she doesn't want to hear about his decisions, which is just as wrong. Pretty soon, they're growing further apart and staying mad at each other all the time. At this point, it's very easy for a third party to be introduced into the relationship.

It's very important for you and your spouse to grow together. Don't allow your mate to outgrow you personally. Make it your business to always keep up with your partner.

Finally, reinforce your personal spiritual life. Your spiritual life is the thread that keeps everything in place. If that's not together, then nothing else will be together. It's important that you keep your commitment to God and your relationship with Him alive. It also helps to have realistic expectations for your mate. But always look to God to meet your expectations, not your spouse.

Chapter 7

The Golden Years: Negotiating The Final Transitions

In a previous chapter, we looked at change in terms of crises. But changes aren't always necessarily critical turning-point incidents. Some changes don't require any decision-making at all. They're just an inevitable part of life. They're simply times of transition that mark the end of one season and the beginning of another.

Menopause, "the empty-nest syndrome," and retirement are three such transitions. But even though they're a normal part of the mid-life experience, they can still be traumatic. So the first thing you need to do is get every bit of information you can about them. That way your faith will have some knowledge behind it. Then you can overcome in these areas.

Menopause

Menopause is the only one of these three changes that happens exclusively to women. The dictionary defines it as *the period of natural cessation of menstruation occurring usually between the ages of 45 and 50.* Some men have been known to experience what is called "male menopause," but obviously it's not the same thing (those occurrences are similar to when a husband gets morning sickness when his wife becomes pregnant).

Men do have biological changes that take place in their bodies, but most males won't talk about what's happening to them, or they'll act as if nothing is happening at all. Even so, the changes in a man are nowhere near the magnitude of the woman's during menopause.

For the woman, menopause marks the transition to later life, and it can be just as dramatic as retirement. When I was younger, I'd hear women complain about it, saying, "It isn't fair. If we have to go through menopause, what do the men have to go through?"

Well, the emotional transition of menopause is for women what retirement is for men. Retirement is very difficult for men because they've basically worked all their lives, and then they're suddenly faced with the reality of not working.

Men who retire voluntarily don't really have a problem since it's a decision that they made. Usually, those men have something else they want to do, anyway. But in the majority of cases, retirement is a very big deal — especially if they're being forced to retire. It's not as big a deal for women, however, which is why retirement the closest experience for men that can be compared to menopause.

Menopause can be a traumatic period in which the woman tends to doubt her own womanhood. It's also a time of mental stress. Many times she won't be thinking straight. That's why she needs the support of her husband. (He may think he's really done something when he learned how to adjust to her menstrual cycle, but he doesn't know that was only practice — just wait until she goes through menopause!)

The woman's body goes through all kinds of hormonal changes during menopause. The chemical substances that naturally occur in her body are all out of balance. That's why she experiences "hot flashes." One minute she's hot; one minute she's cold; and the next minute she's hot and cold both at the same time.

Now, ordinarily, menopause lasts a lot longer than six months, and some women have been known to go through menopause for three or four years. It all depends on your body, how well you handle it, and how much support you have.

When menopause hangs on for a long period of time, it can become a crisis. The thing about these stages of life is that you have to have knowledge of what you're going through. You have to realize that it's going to happen.

The quicker you get out of denial and realize that it's going to happen, the quicker you'll get through it.

It's like a having a baby. If you get pregnant, it's going to happen: You're going to end up on the delivery table! And you don't just decide once you get on the table that you want to have natural childbirth — childbirth without anesthesia or pain medication. It's too late. One thing is sure — you will have a child. Whether it's naturally or not depends on how early you made that decision.

The point is, you have to find out what you need to do in order to be comfortable in the situation.

There are hormone pills that can be prescribed to help alleviate the discomfort that occurs during menopause. Some women refuse to take them. Others swear by them. One lady I know said they were the best things since corn bread!

Someone once asked me if I believed women of faith had to go through hot flashes or any of the other side-effects of menopause, and I said no. I'm basing that on the Word and on my own personal experience.

I had painless childbirth with two of my children. So I know that it *is* possible to go through a physical process that is normally distressing for women and not experience any pain. But you have to have a knowledge of the Word and exercise your faith in God's promises; otherwise you'll perish just like everyone else.

The key to going through this period victoriously is a balance of the spiritual side (standing on God's Word and so forth) and the natural side, which includes getting whatever help and emotional support you need.

The husband can definitely contribute to that balance in a woman's life at this time, because between her having to deal with the menopause that symbolizes the end of her youth and how the world views her age, anyway, she really needs his support. So it's a time when he needs to stand by her, not leave her.

The Empty-Nest Syndrome

Another transition that will inevitably happen is what the world calls "the empty-nest syndrome." It's used to describe the time after children become independent and leave their parents' home. It's not necessarily the point at which they become independent, because many times they can be independent and still be living at home. So it's referring to once they leave home. (If they were still in the nest, then the nest wouldn't be empty, would it?)

Generally, the empty-nest period begins from the departure of the last child to the beginning of retirement, an average of 15 years. It can be a bleak and lonely period, especially for the woman. But in our society, since so many women work, it's not as bleak and lonely for them. By the time some women get home from work, they're tired and don't want to be bothered anyway. So this can be a blessed time for them, in a sense.

Now once you go through the empty-nest syndrome, you're over it. It's when the empty nest and MLC hit at the same time that can be difficult, because you have all sorts of emotions that you're dealing with: the kids are gone; you feel like your spouse has taken you for granted; you don't have anyone depending on you anymore; and so forth. Then if you happen to have children at a late age, by the time your nest is empty, you'll also be going through other transitions, like menopause or retirement. So it can be a difficult time, but the Word can get you through it.

Leaving the Nest

It's a fact of life that your children will have to leave home one day, so you'd better prepare yourself for that day while they're still growing up. You should allow your children a little more freedom at each stage of their lives instead of waiting until they're old enough to be on their own and saying, "All right, you're free now." If you do that, both you and they will have a difficult time with their leaving.

When my son left home for the first time to attend Bible school for two years, I missed him, but I didn't have a difficult time. I grew up in a family of 13 kids and, age-wise, I fell right in the middle. One was already out of the house, but I saw six of my other siblings leave home. So when my son left, it was a very natural thing as far as I was concerned.

People asked me if I was having a hard time with it, and I told them, "No. A child is supposed to leave home." I saw it as normal, because in my own experience I'd had good parents and a good family life.

Now if my son *didn't* want to leave home, *that* would have caused me a problem. Then something would be wrong, because he's supposed to go on and prepare himself for what he needs to be doing next in his life.

My oldest daughter, who is my second child, attended the same Bible school before going on to college, just like her brother did. But I have to admit I had a harder time with her being gone. I think by her being a girl, it was more difficult knowing that she was out there on her own.

You see, even though a daughter leaves the nest, she is still under her daddy's covering. I don't care how old she gets, that responsibility is still there until she gets married and passes from one covering to another. That's why it's so important for a father to be in agreement with the relationship his daughter commits to. He has to be willing to pass his covering over to another man.

So I believe that it can be more difficult when girls leave home, because you have to be more active in their lives.

When our son left, we weren't tempted to call him every day, and it didn't bother us if he wasn't home when we did call. But it bothers us when our daughter isn't home and doesn't answer her voice mail. But that's all part of the empty-nest experience.

Letting Go — Accepting Your Changing Roles

A large part of getting through the empty-nest syndrome is just learning how to let go and allow your children to stand on their own. That means coming to terms with your shifting roles as parents and realizing that if you've put in them what you were supposed to put in them, they'll be all right.

Again, that's why it's so important to teach your children the Word and how to exercise their faith when they're growing up. By that, I don't mean just *telling* them but *living* it before them in the home. Children learn by precept *and* example!

You'll know that you've done your job when you see your children start to take on the roles you once had in their lives. For example, my husband and I always lived a lifestyle of faith in the home; so our children learned that faith works. Our youngest daughter is still at the "give me all you want to give me" stage (we're still working on her), but our two oldest children are at the place where they pretty much want to use their own faith for things.

Our oldest daughter told us that she didn't want us to buy her a car unless the Lord told us to. We understood where she was coming from, but I told her, "Look, if your daddy buys you the car that you want, then you'd better believe God moved on his heart! That's the *only* way you'd get that kind of car out of him!" (She was believing God for a sporty luxury import!)

First of all, we had to make sure that her motives were right, because many times when you're in ministry, people will pressure your children just because they're blessed. Folks will tell them things such as, "You don't have it as hard because you have people who are supporting you."

So we had to check to see where she was coming from. But her response was still that she didn't want it if God didn't move on our hearts to do it. She wanted to use her faith. It excites her to see the manifestation of her faith in operation.

Sometimes you'll find once your children get out on their own, they resent it if you try to do something for them or they feel that you're trying to dictate to them what they get in life. So you have just have to leave them alone at that point.

You need to realize that you no longer have the control over their lives that you were accustomed to having. That in itself takes some adjusting to. You won't be able to bless them and do things for them the way you used to, because they want to be able to do things for themselves and stand on their own.

Now, when the "empty nest" hits, suddenly, you

have access to all this money — money that you used to spend on your children — and you have to find somewhere else to put it. So I guess you have to wait until those grandkids come along. No one can stop you from blessing *them*!

Once your children go out and start families of their own, you can't force yourself on them. You become their extended family, so you can't do for them like you would if they were in your home. You have to respect their decisions, step back, and allow them the opportunity to let their families develop.

It can be very difficult to have to suddenly take a back seat when you've spent half your life raising your children and being a family to them. But if you understand and respect God's order, then you won't have as hard a time.

One reason why some people have such a hard time with this is that they don't have anything else to do. They don't have a life anymore. Their lives were wrapped up in their kids.

Well, if you do it God's way, your life is going to be wrapped up primarily in your spouse. Everything else which comes out of that relationship, children included, is just a blessing. Then when you reach the empty-nest stage, you're blessed even more, because you see your grown children beginning their own lives and you realize that you did something right. (It's always a blessing to know you've done things the way that God ordained.)

Your role as a parent was bound to change, so during this time, you should be readjusting your priorities. Your commitment to your spouse will always be your first priority, but spending time with your children will no longer have the same place. The whole focus in your home shifts back to just you and your spouse.

So, really, you need to look at the empty-nest period as a good thing. It's simply a time of transition. It's meant to be a time of adjustment. It's a good time to reexamine your marriage to see if you've reached the goals you set as a couple. It's also the time to renegotiate your marriage and begin a new partnership. You need to find out where you want to go next and what you need to do in order to get there. Then you can work on banding closer together and preparing for the next season in your marriage.

You may discover that you have to reestablish the feelings and love you once had for each other. But you'll also find that you have more freedom to do it. You can walk around the house again with nothing on if you want to! You don't have to lock your bedroom door anymore. You don't even have to take the phone off the hook.

All the things you couldn't do when your

children were there, you now have the liberty to enjoy once again. So you should use this time to reestablish the importance of your marriage and to rediscover one another. You can renew or fortify your relationship and experience even greater intimacy than you had before. If you'll take advantage of this time, you'll find that you'll be in a much better position to face the retirement years ahead.

Retirement

As the years pass by, not only will the children go, but the bills will too. (Your money adds up when you don't have to spend it on your children anymore.) This is especially true if you saved and exercised "delayed gratification" while you were young.

In other words, if you waited and saved up money to purchase things instead of buying them up front, you probably have everything you want by now — and debt-free!

For example, in the ideal situation, your house is paid off, you've finished putting your kids through college, and you have enough money set aside to buy a car (with cash!) if you wanted to. So everything is pretty much in place. But you may start to reevaluate your life at this point and think, *Why am I working so hard then? I have plenty of money. I don't need to do all this.*

When children are no longer in the home, people sometimes go through a time of reassessment when they ask themselves, *Do I really need to work anymore?* That's usually when they decide if they want to retire, take a sabbatical, or whatever. This happens many times in cases where the woman was only working to help out with the bills.

But whether the decision to retire is voluntary or involuntary, there's a sense of loss that accompanies it.

If your reason for working was to provide for your family and do the best you could for your employer, then once the children are out of the picture and your employer is gone, you might lose your sense of meaning and purpose or struggle with feelings of no longer being useful to society. That's why you need to retire *to* something instead of *from* something.

Volunteering Your Services

If you've worked all your life and now you're being kicked out of the work force, go volunteer somewhere a couple of days a week.

The beauty about volunteering is that you can set your own hours. If you want, you can sleep late and go in at one o' clock in the afternoon. Even if you only volunteer for two hours a day, at least you'll feel useful, because you're doing something and someone is depending on you.

Some people get a part-time job or volunteer after they retire simply because they need to get out of the house. It's not so much that they feel useless, but they need something to do. They've worked all their lives and now, all of a sudden, they're expected to sit back and do nothing, and they just can't handle it.

No one who is retired should ever complain of being bored, because there are all kinds of things to do and so many people who need help. When you're retired, you can help out in the church more.

People look at the retirement world and think that you're not supposed to do anything when you're retired. No, retirement means that you don't have to work for some other person any longer. You can do what you want to do now. You can spend your time doing the work of the ministry or volunteering your services at a local school, library, or hospital.

Nursing homes are a perfect place to volunteer since there are so many neglected elderly people staying in them. Those old folks don't care if they know you, just as long as they can talk to you. You might have to wear earplugs though, because they'll talk and talk and talk. Most of them are starved for attention!

If you don't like being around older people, you can visit the pediatric wards at a local hospital or medical clinic. It's a shame how many children are left alone in those facilities because their parents aren't able to be there to watch out for them.

Personally, I believe that someone should stay there all the time when your loved one is a patient, especially when it's an elderly person or a child, because sometimes patients can be mistreated or even neglected. (My mother experienced that when she had to be hospitalized once.)

I have a nephew who was born a preemie, and he would have died if my sister had left him alone at the hospital. His lungs hadn't completely developed, so he had to stay on a respirator until he was healthy enough to go home. While he was there in the CCU, someone accidentally kicked the plug out of his respirator and he wasn't getting any oxygen. No one on the staff had noticed. But my sister stayed right there with him all the time, and, thank God, she was able to immediately discover that there was a problem.

The nurses aren't always paying attention

because they're busy running around, doing what they have to do. So you can spend time with those who are hospitalized and be a blessing and a comfort to them while they're there alone.

Besides hospitals, there are plenty of community organizations or activities you can get involved with. But find something to do. Don't just sit around.

Now even though you never retire from the ministry, there will come a time when you do retire, generally speaking. So if you know that time is coming, you need to start preparing for it. Don't be like some people who keep putting retirement off until sometime in the future. Then when the time comes, they're totally unprepared.

Why not spend the years leading up to retirement developing yourself personally and spiritually? Explore new interests or hobbies. Work on building up your relationship with your spouse. Start seeking God ahead of time concerning what He has planned for you during that season of your life. That way, you'll have a general idea what you're going to do when the time comes.

If you plan for your retirement, it will be a blessing for you when it comes rather than a curse. Then instead of nagging your spouse and making things worse, you'll be working together toward a common goal. You won't have time to entertain thoughts such as, *I haven't grown, I don't have any other interests,* or *I don't know what to do now that the kids are gone,* because you're not looking back — you're too busy looking at what's ahead!

Enjoy Your New Season

A Christian has no business looking back, anyway. What are you going to look back for? You can't change the things that are behind you. So just forget them and keep pressing forward to the new seasons of life that God has for you.

> **ECCLESIASTES 3:1 (*Amplified*)**
> **1 To every thing there is a season, and a time for every matter or purpose under heaven.**

When you've been obedient to God, you can look forward with excitement and great anticipation to each new season in life that He gives you. God always brings us into a wider place. You'll be blessed going in and blessed going out (Deut. 28:6).

You can't help but be blessed when you've been a good steward over the two most prized relationships that God has entrusted to you — the marriage and family.

There is a blessing in developing a total

marriage and maintaining harmony in your home. There's a blessing in knowing that you've produced godly seed and that your children are bringing up their children in the ways of the Lord. There's a blessing in being able to follow God's will for your life in ministry *with* your family instead of at their expense.

But the biggest blessing of all has to be the joy of coming full circle in your journey with a lifetime of rich memories and a mate who's still committed, still loving, and still standing by your side.

About the Author

Mrs. Deborah L. Butler is the first lady of Word of Faith International Christian Center in Southfield, Michigan, Word of Faith Christian Center in Akron, Ohio, and Faith Christian Center in Phoenix, Arizona, where she serves in the ministry with her husband, Bishop Keith A. Butler. She is a licensed and ordained minister of the Gospel.

Minister Deborah Butler is the director of Women of Virtue, an organization which promotes fellowship among women and ministers the Word of God to them, bringing healing and restoration to many. Through this organization, Minister Butler helps women realize who they are in Christ and how to walk in the wisdom of God, experiencing peace in every area of their lives.

Emphasizing marriage and the family in her teaching, Minister Butler presents the Word in a skillful, yet down-to-earth manner, imparting wisdom to all who hear and helping them deal scripturally with the many issues of life that confront them.

Minister Butler is also an instructor at Word of Faith Bible Training Center and the administrative assistant at Word of Faith International Christian Center. She and her husband have three children, Rev. Keith A. Butler, II, Minister MiChelle Butler, and Ms. Kristina Butler, and a daughter-in-law, Minister Tiffany Butler.

Other Titles
By Word of Faith Publishing

Bishop Keith A. Butler

Pastor Keith A. Butler

The Prosperous Touch:
Gaining Financial Freedom   BK052
God's Plan For the Single Saint   BK006
For PK's Only: A Book for the Next
Generation (Rev. Keith A. Butler II
   and Min. MiChelle Butler)   BK016
The Right Way To Give   BK033
God Is Making You Rich   BK018

Min. Deborah L. Butler

Establishing Godly Relationships
Through Marriage and Family   BK012

Min. MiChelle A. Butler

The Glass Rose   BK028
Self-Esteem   BK023